Good word

MW00427689

"Wheth g ...., facing a
serious diagnosis, overcoming the feeling of being
alone or coming to terms with your beliefs about
God, life takes courage. Healing for each of these
— or other mental, physical, emotional or spiritual
wounds — follows the same process. Meagan beau-
tifully lays out the steps for readers as she unfolds
her own story. You will see yourself in her struggles,
and in her triumphs, and you too, will heal."

—Tracy Maxwell, Author of *Being Single, with
Cancer: A Solo Survivor's Guide to Life, Love, Health &
Happiness*

*Jeann —
To Courage
and more...*

Meagan M. O'Nan

COURAGE

Agreeing
To Disagree
Is Not Enough

Copyright © 2014 Meagan M. O'Nan
Meagan O'Nan
www.couragethebridgetofreedom.com
or contact at:
140 Brickerton Street
Columbus, MS 39701

Copyright ©2014 Meagan M. O'Nan

All rights reserved. Including the right of reproduction in whole or part
in any form. No part of this book may be reproduced in any form or by
any electronic means including information storage and retrieval systems
without the written permission from the author, except for brief passages
embodied in articles and reviews.

First edition, 2014
ISBN: 978-1-4951-2459-4
Library of Congress Control Number: 2014914935
Edited by Clare Mallory O'Nan
Designed by Toolbox Creative
Printed and bound in The United States of America

For Joan.

Even when you don't have a church to go to, even when you aren't sure how your family feels about who you are, even when you don't have a stable community to stand around you...even then, you are strong enough. The depth of who you are and the courage you have within are big enough to carry you until you see that you were surrounded by love the entire time, and that you deserve it. The resilience of the human spirit is so overwhelmingly profound that it can take the pounding that life challenges it with. We can truly get through anything, and if you know that about yourself then the tough conversations, the heartbreaks, the losses, and the unknowns become a part of life's magnificence so that the joyful moments are enhanced more and more with every new step. The bottom line is this: you are stronger than you could ever imagine and you are worthy of every ounce of love that makes its way to you. Courage gives you the ability to look within and transform your pain into love so that there is no desire to disagree with another.

—Meagan M. O'Nan

❧ Table of Contents

Foreword

"You are a really gifted writer whose style is very straight-forward, engaging and clean."

These are the words I sent to Meagan O'Nan via email when I first began reading *Courage*. It was my initial impression as I turned the pages.

However, prior to reading Meagan's book, I had already begun to see her as a prominent voice for our times. I had become absorbed in her blog posts chronicling her journey from an anxious woman who thought she might be gay to her embrace of the fact that she is. The posts began to form a body of work where her words expressed not only her fears and self-judgment, but her frustrations at societal perceptions, which were becoming more vocal and critical in the context of current events.

It is crucial to see Meagan's work against this backdrop. At this pivotal moment in our nation's – and world's – history, Meagan has stepped up with something vital to say about love, compassion, commitment and, by extension, civil rights. This book is a poignant and powerful reminder that there are human beings with the desire to love at the heart of what is too often an impersonal political or religious debate. Real people, real feelings, real faces affected by the legislation, the doctrine and the disparaging remarks directed at people we may not understand. Meagan is real and she represents anyone who was raised to believe that there is something wrong with who they are.

This isn't a story of victimhood. It doesn't set out to convert or convince. It's a sharing experience. Whatever your sexual orientation, race, gender, religion, political affiliation or ethnicity, this is a relatable story. Meagan uses her writing gift to show us, in this moment, why change is afoot and why that's a beautiful thing.

We as a people are breaking through archaic mindsets that restrict and condemn. First it was little by little, but now it is more sweeping. We are opening a window, letting in the air and the freshness. It is a new day. I like the idea of Meagan helping to usher it in for us. I like that she states – as opposed to rails or preaches – and that she reaches conclusions based on deep thinking and self-examination.

The reader gets unfiltered access to Meagan's insights as they unfold in her own life. She takes readers on her quest for answers with all the lumps and setbacks that come with that. She freely acknowledges shifts in her own thinking. This is what she used to think; this is what she thinks now. She is teaching through living, something that will likely continue as long as she draws breath.

"To make our lives meaningful takes courage," wrote the Dalai Lama in a foreword for a book called *Learning to Breathe.*

It is apt here. Meagan is on that quest.

Through spiritual and emotional avenues, an opening to love and a willingness to buck even her own self-flagellating mindset, she has arrived at a place where peace is actually possible. Note I didn't say she has reached inner peace. What she has reached is another level of understanding and self-acceptance, quite the sound foundation for inner peace.

In another email, I wrote this impression to Meagan:

"I think the overarching theme/lesson is you recognizing—over and over again—your own power. And that it will continue for the rest of your life."

Indeed.

With love. With patience. With courage.

—Nancy Colasurdo (July 2014) Writer/Coach

A Call For Courage

"Courage is not the absence of fear, but rather the judgment that something else is more important than fear"
—Ambrose Redmoon

I am a woman who is gay and who is from Mississippi. In my first book, "Creating Your Heaven on Earth," I threw that detail out on page 110 very subtly. At that point in my life (five years ago), I was ashamed of who I was, so I feared to be too bold. I wanted people to know but I didn't. So I put it deep into a chapter for a couple of paragraphs and knew it was possible that most people would never even read it. At the time, I didn't know it was shame—I was just trying to survive.

I'm not sure of all the reasons why, but over the years I have found the courage within to be okay with a lot of who I am. Somehow, I have been able to see past the "not good enough" label and have stopped allowing myself to be shoved under the rug or become the elephant in the room. Not that the "not good enough because I am gay" tape in my mind has stopped completely, but I have learned to listen when it shows up and how to move through it.

After being gone from Mississippi for many years, I eventually returned. I have had some pretty tough conversations since then, have learned how to introduce my partner in public with joy, and have even begun to believe in myself. It hasn't been easy. I don't think it is easy for anyone to live an authentic life, but I am doing it the best way I know how. In the end, I found the courage I had always been looking for, but I found it in the oddest place — inside of me. If I hadn't put in a conscious effort to discover that, I would not be sitting here writing this book.

For a while now, I've set aside a lot of time to figure out and embrace my own voice. I have asked myself many times, "Who are you and what do you want to leave behind?" But I soon came to realize that if I continued to focus on leaving something behind I may miss out on who I am.

For ten years, there has been an internal struggle of self-defeat within me that I have been trying to overcome. I have chiseled away at it consciously for about five years now. A part of my spirit has been wanting to shine its light, and yet there has been a part of me saying, "You aren't ready yet." Patience has been the key to my own healing. Patience is hard. Faith is harder. And courage is the toughest.

It is really hard when you are the type of person who was once a successful athlete —the type of person who always achieved what she wanted easily —and then you stop achieving. I stopped achieving things easily when I came out of the closet ten years ago. Life became hard after that, a struggle, but what I didn't realize was that the struggle wasn't ever that I couldn't achieve; it was that I had lost my voice.

Believing that I was a failure because I am gay has been the driving force behind all my hesitations for years. Ironically, losing my voice was due to this very belief. If I believe I am a failure, then that is what I will be, no matter what I may ever accomplish. Thank goodness I now know that I am not a failure and that there is nothing wrong with me. I knew it all along in my brain, somewhere up there, but to actually embrace myself —a totally different story.

Within the past year, I have heard some sad stories about people in the gay community here in Mississippi. Marco McMillan of Clarksdale, who would have been the first openly gay politician in Mississippi, was murdered this year at the age of 34. At such a young age, his death hit home for me. It brought up every fear I have ever had as a gay woman from Mississippi. At around the same time, two women in Laurel,

Mississippi, decided to get married. They made it to the front page of the newspaper, which was a proud moment for our history as a state; however, the larger community responded with great outrage.

Both of these stories offer an opportunity for us all to think about what kind of person we want to be in the world. Behind the fear that they both invoke in me (and possibly in most gay Mississippians), I feel pushed to find my voice...a voice that is not motivated by fear but by love.

I know I want to be a person who has a voice for the things that are most important to me. Not a voice that condemns, but a voice that resonates with everyone. It's hard enough to have a conversation about what is really going on —not talking about it at all can't be an option. And we certainly can't have conversations when one person or both people are screaming.

Courage is having those tough conversations. One of the biggest gifts for me in the process of accepting who I am has been the open and honest conversations that I have had with my parents. We would never be where we are if we had not all been willing to be honest about where we were on our journey. Conversations lead to understanding, and understanding leads to acceptance, and acceptance leads to forgiveness, and forgiveness leads to healing, and healing leads to seeing ourselves in the other. When we finally get to a place where we see ourselves in those in front of us, then fear can take a back seat and love can become the driver of a giant bus called "Moving Forward." Love is a choice. Trust is a choice.

I had a blog for a while called *Everyone's Gay! Straight Talk about Discrimination* that I eventually let go of because something more "normal" came my way. Actually, it was fear that drove me to drop the blog, but I didn't recognize that until much later. Well, normal didn't work for me for very long, as I found myself bored out of my mind doing work I found unfulfilling. I fell into doing what I thought I "should" be doing (i.e., not writing about my experiences of being gay) rather than what I wanted to do. I have since been taking my time, looking behind my own layers of fear and failure so that I could find the real me...the me that knows that nothing is wrong with who I am, the me that knows everything is right with who I am. The me that sees my fear and knows that I am courageous.

In order to find courage I had to go to that deep dark place that we all know–the place where doubt, lack of self-love and self-worthiness, and fear of the unknown reside. I had to dive into the dark in order to find myself, and I think that is the only way to do it–dive in and let the rest unfold. Now, whether you are a person who believes that being gay is a sin or a person who believes in gay marriage, don't close the book just yet. I have a lot to say — not to point the finger, to blame, to claim who is right and who is wrong, but to see that perhaps we can rise higher than we ever have before. I know we can, because I have been able to in my own life. And if I have the courage, then I know you do.

"Courage" is a book that has been growing inside of me my entire life, like a seed that was planted when I was born, only to grow slowly and patiently in its own time despite my desire for it to hurry along. Although I have always wanted to write about my true thoughts and beliefs about truth, equality, and love as I have come to know them, the Universe has been taking its time sowing the seed within me. This book has gone through five different titles and has been in the works for several years. I knew it would develop in its own time, and I also knew that my own healing and willingness to look at my own life and struggles would eventually get me to a place where the time was right for this book to be completed. My competitive spirit and the rush I have felt to make a difference before I die have been trumped by a timing which is not my own. I have come to know that true courage is all about being who you really are and not just talking about it.

I have often questioned, more than I would like to admit, if my offerings will matter, if they will be valued or if they will help others (a question I think we all ask), and if my pain has been real enough for me to finally acknowledge it out loud. It is in these questions that I found my answer: I will never know the answer. I do not claim to know any more about life than anyone else.

My dreams for myself have always been similar to the dreams that most people have: to express my heart in a way that makes my soul sing in service to the world. I have gotten to know my soul in brief moments along the way, and the common denominator of these moments has always been when I have chosen to rise above my doubts about myself in order to see the other. To sway away from suffering means diving into my own wounds, so that I transform from a small seed into a big oak tree. I have learned quickly that clenching my fists doesn't allow space for love to enter, and if love never enters then I cannot know myself, and I certainly cannot begin to know others.

Although all of us are familiar with injustice, a feeling that is desperate, empty, and larger than words, we often find comfort in the illusion of feeling in control —until the next injustice approaches. Just as an alcoholic is always looking for the next drink, we too are always looking for the next person to speak against us or to make us feel less than. We then take that experience to turn it against the other person so that we can feel in control again. We humans have spent much of our history ignoring our true nature by claiming that one group is better than the other, and that pattern will continue to repeat itself until each of us is able to love those closest to us —those we often perceive as the most threatening. I believe that part of our learning process is to inject ourselves into the bigger picture, and that when we grasp for control of the unfolding universe we end up making it smaller, only to find despair, loneliness, and hopelessness there.

I am not saying that if you read this book you will rise out of victimhood and suddenly live the victorious life you are wanting. I am saying that this is the way I have chosen and the way that has worked for me. Most importantly, it is an offering to give hope that the healing process is possible and that rising out of your own limitations is doable.

In March 2013, a series of Supreme Court hearings began that related to gay marriage rights in the United States. I remember having a lot of emotions as the hearings got started. The majority of what I was feeling was anxiety. My anxiety was a combination of fear and excitement wrapped together. I really was hopeful that the fear would subside so that anticipation and hope could step forward, but that meant I would have to be willing to see the best in all people: myself, my parents, my family, my friends, the State of Mississippi, and beyond —gay and straight alike. As a gay woman from Mississippi who had

had a really tough coming-out experience, that was a risk for me. Still, I wanted to use this experience to uncover more of who I am, and so I was willing to put aside my fears so that that truth could really seep in.

At the time, I had been reading a lot about the dangers of being openly gay in Mississippi, and without realizing it I had forgotten to keep my eyes open and embrace my own positive experience. I had been living in my own past and at the same time wishing to move out of it, and realizing it was up to me to release it.

Letting love in is hard for me. Really hard. Asking for support is even harder. I learned around that time that my dad proudly introduces Clare (my partner of almost five years) as my partner to others. This was a surprise to me—in the South, it's one thing to embrace each other behind closed doors, but in public? I felt so seen, so heard, so important. Around that time, my mom acknowledged how tough it must have been for me when I came out of the closet and how brave I was to come back to Mississippi—and it was hard to let that in because a part of me had been waiting for the other shoe to drop. I saw clearly that it was time for me to move on. To let go.

Although Clare and I were "in a relationship" on Facebook, introducing her to new people as my partner had been a struggle for me, and very inconsistent. I usually liked to measure someone up to see if I thought they would be "cool" with it or not. I slowly began to see that that wasn't fair to me, to them, or to Clare. Every day, I felt like I had to self-talk up my courage to go out into the world and be ready to be authentic. I was really tired of prepping – really tired of worrying.

Believing in myself and believing in the best of others is what I had been putting in my heart each day – consciously trying to put my shield down and open my heart. But when society – or better said, when I believe that society (here in the South) – is against who I am, it's tough to see the light in each person, to let them into my world without wanting to run and hide. When you're so used to lying about who you are, lying becomes a habit. And even now that I know being authentic is my only choice, I have to admit that sometimes it's easier to say "no" to social events than be uncomfortable. It's too painful to not tell the whole truth.

So the Supreme Court hearings brought up a lot for me. When someone asks me, "Are you married?" it's easier to say, "No," rather than, "No, but only because I can't" – which could lead to a richer conversation and a deeper connection. But when I answer "No," I feel defeated, I feel like a liar, and I feel like I am choosing the easy way out — and then it's so easy to spiral into self-defeat. This is a struggle for me at times, and I continually work on it.

The weekend before the hearings, Clare and I went to get a haircut. There were a total of five of us there in the salon, and we were all making small talk. One woman was getting ready to leave (I didn't know her), and she asked me if Clare and I were friends or sisters. I took a run around my head first, which told me to be completely honest, and I said, "No, actually, Clare is my partner." And I felt confident. I felt liberated. I felt like there was nothing to apologize for because there's not. We are who we are. The woman said, "Oh, okay," and then went on to ask questions about sports. It didn't matter that she wasn't enamored with our relationship—what mattered was that I was authentic and that I wasn't feeling the need to explain myself. I didn't feel that deep dark hole of doubt creeping in. I felt victorious! (And then I think, there's something wrong when just answering a simple question honestly turns into such a victory — it shouldn't be a victory just to say who you are.)

Afterwards, I thought, now why has this been such a difficult feat for me? Put me on NPR and I will tell you my story of coming out in Mississippi; put me on TV and I will talk with a Southern Baptist preacher about being gay in Mississippi (you will read about these two stories later on in the book); put me in front of a crowded room—no problem, gay and proud. But one-on-one? A completely different story. That's when any shame or fear I have rises up to my mouth and the words I speak aren't a lie, but they aren't the truth either. Head down. Defeat.

Is all of this my fault? Is my internal struggle of acceptance something I have done to myself? I mean, I know that Mississippi isn't packed full of a victorious progressive history, but I am choosing to live here, so shouldn't I be taking the blame? No, I don't think so, at least not completely. I am just as responsible as everyone else.

For us all to experience love and acceptance, it is going to take me continuing to have the courage to be truthful in those one-on-one conversations, and it's going to take a lot more people like my dad speaking matter-of-factly about Clare being my partner. It's going to take courage on my part to grab Clare's hand in public when I feel compelled, and not let go when someone looks our way. It's going to take all of us. Me and you.

It's going to take parents like my parents who cheer for me when I tell them I was able to be honest with someone I didn't know in a one-on-one conversation today. It's going to take friends stepping up when their friendships are challenged. It's going to take more than me finding the courage to be me every day—it's going to take all of my goodhearted

Mississippians, fellow Americans, and all people of the world to reach out and put our arms around each other.

Connection is one of the most important things about being human, it's what makes shame disappear and what makes our history turn for the better. We all need it—we all crave it. That includes me. And you.

It isn't about being gay. It's about whatever we use to make ourselves "less than." It isn't easy for me — or for anyone else, either. Everyone is scared on some level. But when I think about what's possible, I can see through the smoke to the light...the light that is waiting for us to love ourselves enough, and our fellow people enough, to be courageous, to be supportive, to be authentic—from the inside out.

In the end, aren't we all tired of fear? I am. My story is around Mississippi and the pain I have experienced here, but I am letting it go so I can see it for what it is. Mississippi: A courageous, beautiful, complicated, loving mess where love can rise above the mess to make me a better me if I allow it to.

We all have our Mississippis. We all have places and people that have hurt us deeply. But we have to move beyond political agendas, religious power, social acceptance, the need to be right, the need to make others wrong, and the need to be okay with agreeing to disagree, and instead act on really loving each other the way we all want and desire to be loved. I have learned to put my armor down. The laws themselves might change, but it is ultimately up to us to make change happen.

While a lot of my story and experiences are a result of being gay and all the insecurities, fears, and challenges that it has brought me, this book is more about how we as human beings feel we have been oppressed in our own lives; and it challenges us to look at how we are now oppressing others. It takes tremendous courage to look within and transform our own pain into love so that we are able to feel equal to all.

This book is an offering of hope, an offering for others to see that you can believe in yourself again and that your own courage is waiting for you to give it a voice; that by believing in yourself you do not feel a need to tell others how to live their lives. It takes a great amount of courage and commitment to look within instead of looking outside of yourself for answers. It may take time and a willingness to grow, but the seed is in each one of us, and it is possible.

Strong people cry sometimes, fall sometimes and feel like giving up sometimes, but what makes them strong is that they keep on going anyway.

—Sonya Parker

CHAPTER 1

My Story: How I Have Come To Know Courage

*All my life I had been looking for something, and every-
where I turned someone tried to tell me what it was. I
accepted their answers too, though they were often in
contradiction and even self-contradictory. I was naïve.
I was looking for myself and asking everyone except
myself questions which I, and only I, could answer. It
took me a long time and much painful boomeranging
of my expectations to achieve a realization everyone
else appears to have been born with: that I am nobody
but myself.*

—Ralph Ellison

I have come to know courage intimately over the years.
I have called on it in ways that may seem brave to others, and
I have called on it in moments when most think you wouldn't
need courage to overcome something. The courage within me
has taught me first that I cannot and will not be broken, and
second that I do not want to and will not break others.

My true nature is to be authentic to who I am, and who
I am happens to include being gay. I therefore learned very
quickly that in order to deal with those who openly think that
being gay is a sin I had to first heal everything inside of me
that was telling me I wasn't good enough. Then, once I started
to feel good about who I was, I saw that I couldn't authentically
put others down even if they were putting me down.

I have studied some of the greats (Nelson Mandela,
Gandhi, Jesus) on how to handle controversies that were playing themselves out in my own life – how to rise above injustice
when the majority of those around me may not even realize
the injustice is happening. The answer that I've found, and
which I have come to know so intimately, is that I must find a
way to continue to love myself, to break down my own barriers
against love so that I can love others freely, with no attach-
ment and no desire of wanting to please them. Tough? Yes.
Doable? Absolutely. I may not be totally there yet, and I may
never get there, but I will strive to, each and every day. Let me

tell you more about my own journey and how I have come to know courage.

When I was 8 years old, I woke my mom in the middle of the night saying, "I am afraid that eternity will end. What if it ends and then we don't exist any longer?" The feeling was terrifying and overwhelming — I couldn't wrap my mind around my own existence, let alone our existence as a whole. She couldn't give me an answer, but she could hold me, love me, and comfort me. I believe she was always dumbfounded by my questions, but it was in her comforting and in her love that I began to scratch the surface of who I am, of who we all are.

I have seen and learned that love is the answer to most questions, as well as to the question I had at 8 years of age. Now, at 31 years of age, I am able to somewhat understand that that same emptiness I feared at 8 is the vastness in which we all are, and within that vastness is our capacity to love, forgive, and accept beyond fulfillment. If we combine all that is alive in the universe and each person's and each being's capacity to love into one, can you imagine the possibilities? Inside that universe of capability are you and I...inside our chest and in the depths of our souls is the light we all seek to embrace, the capability that is both within us and beyond us. I do believe we can embrace the light within us by embracing the courage we have to transform ourselves.

I have seen the truth of ourselves in many great lead-
ers before me: Nelson Mandela, Elie Wiesel, Jesus, Gandhi,
Martin Luther King, Jr., Abraham Lincoln, Cesar Chavez,
Mother Teresa, to name a few. We have been shown over and
over that we are capable of greater love and greater understanding, and yet we struggle against one another, hoping the
other will change so we will feel safe and secure. In some odd
way we find it easier to hold onto our own ways than transform
into a more fulfilling joy, and thus we often miss the opportunity to dive into our light and realize a slight drop of who we
really are.

Being a woman who is gay and from Mississippi, I have
had my own internal and external battles with confidence. My
hope in myself and in others has been repeatedly tested, and
my faith in the world has been uprooted, ripped apart, and
re-planted. When I decided to openly admit that I was gay, I
slowly closed my heart to the world so I wouldn't feel the pain.
I think everyone has that moment, and not enough are willing to look within enough to transform their pain into love.
Moving a mountain within takes silence, consistency, and a
preparedness to be wrong.

Growing up, I was shy, introverted, and confused by
Mississippian society. As an athlete, I was able to express myself
in ways that made me feel alive and as though I had a purpose.

I was a great student, and I remember always striving to be the best person I could be. I was always looking for people I could help or inspire, always looking for ways to boost someone's confidence. Meaningful friendships were important to me at a young age, and I never made time for friendships that felt "fake." I was honored over and over again for my accomplishments and began to become accustomed to being a standout of sorts.

After high school, I dreamed of playing basketball at Mississippi State University, so I did. I also went on to play softball at Mississippi State University. At that time, I was open to life and knew deep down that if I wanted something it would happen naturally. I never stood in the way of myself, and if I was challenged to get better as an athlete, student, or person, then I faced the challenge. I forced myself to grow in every area of my life because it was important to me, and I had this resounding faith that everything always worked out.

Then came the time when all of my beliefs, and all of the love I had inside, were questioned. I could never have predicted it, but I do think that we all have this moment in our lives...a defining moment that will either propel us forward into new and greater depths of who we are, or stifle our growth and deaden our existence. A moment when pain hits our path, breaking us and forcing us to spend our entire lives revisiting its wounds, or pushing us to dig deeper and find more of ourselves and the love we have inside.

When we are given complete freedom and independence to choose how we will live, we begin to decide who we want to be in the world. For most of us, this happens around the time we graduate high school. We all come into this time feeling like we can save the world from despair, and many of us try to do just that. With this sudden rush of freedom, we feel like we can accomplish anything. While our parents' voices are usually a phone call away by this point, we know we can overcome their doubts with action. Or at least, there is a spirit within us that we feel supersedes our parents' wants for us. The battle within begs the question, "Who do I really want to be in the world?"

We all grow up being taught, whether consciously or unconsciously, to live the way our parents live, and we learn those ways and adopt them as our own. Once we reach this stage of freedom in our late teens or early twenties, we start to see that maybe we are not like our parents, and so there is this moment when everything clashes. Not that our parents were necessarily wrong in how they raised us, but we have a yearning and craving to know who we really are and what that means to us as an individual.

The moment that broke me was when I told my family that I was gay. I was 22 at the time. Perhaps your moment is when you tell your family that you don't want to run the family business, or when you decide to leave the religion that you grew up with, or marry someone of another race. Or maybe it is when you tell your family that you want to live across the world or go into the army. Whatever you tell your family that is not in alignment with what they want you to be, is that moment.

My experience, initially, was very painful. I had always been the "good girl," and this confession broke the mold of who I had been so far, for me and for my family and even my friends. Even as I write this, I can see that there is a part of me that still feels "bad" and "wrong" for being gay. I had a rough coming-out process all the way around. Basically, the whole experience broke my heart into pieces. I lost hope in everyone, and most importantly, I lost hope in who I was.

Coming out to my family was a train wreck. Mom cried, dad was confused, my older brother told me I should move from Mississippi because he thought it would be safer for me, and my little brother just didn't have much to say. The groups of people I had been surrounded and supported by began to attack me and act like all I had been was gone forever. And in some sense, I began losing myself too. I was learning to think that who I was, was wrong, and that I was no longer good enough for what I wanted out of life.

At the time, I was a two-sport athlete at Mississippi State University, playing in my own hometown of Starkville, Mississippi. It was my dream to play sports at Mississippi State, and in the middle of my dream, I was suddenly crushed. Being an academic All-American standout, a National Strength and Conditioning All-American, and the recipient of several community service awards, a person who was known in the community for her efforts to never give up, I suddenly felt alone and exposed, with only inconvenient memories of what everyone else had conveniently forgotten.

I had been a member of the Fellowship of Christian Athletes on campus for years, and it was the foundation of many friendships that I had at the time. As soon as the word got out that I was gay, I received hate voicemails and was ignored and shunned by many, and several sat me down to remind me that I was sure to go to hell. I would often lie and tell them that I wasn't in a relationship with a woman anymore just so they would leave me alone. I wasn't okay with being a liar, but I just wanted to survive. I learned to lie well, which was a tactic I used to cope over the years. What I went through was abuse—no one should ever have to hear that who they are isn't okay.

My entire senior season with softball, I played with a broken foot and never once complained. I look back on that with fondness because it reminds me that I am strong and that

I know how to dig deep when I need to. Luckily, the professors and a few friends in my counseling graduate program reached out and embraced me. They allowed me an opportunity to grieve and to be consoled. I felt like I was being stomped on in all directions, so to have a saving grace somewhere made me feel a little less alone.

At some point, my mom gave me a stack of papers about a fix-it camp that she thought I could go to. She was desperate to understand and so afraid for me, but the sight of the papers in front of me made the rejection feel even more impossible to deal with. I remember crying tears of desperation at night, hoping that God would shine down on me and give me a reason for why He made me this way. Some thought I was doing it to be a rebel, but I had never liked attention and had always had high moral and ethical character. I felt bad immediately if I began to gossip — or even if I was around it, I never did drugs or smoked a cigarette (nor did I ever want to, even at my lowest point), I attended church as often as I could (more than once a week), I held empowerment Bible studies for women athletes and brought groups of friends together every week for dinner at my parents' house...I was living a good life and doing everything "right," but all of that seemed to disappear from their memories once they heard I was gay.

I had been in my first real relationship with a woman for a year by now. During that whole senior year, my grades hadn't slipped; in fact, they had gone up. My performance in softball was at its peak. Life should have been good. But I was keeping a secret from everyone and it was killing me. I always ran to my pen and paper to express the depth of my sadness. With my mom unable to connect with me because she was confused, I was at a loss for who to talk to...she had always been the one that I had talked to. My dad was angry and confused, concerned that I would go to hell, and he wouldn't engage with me either. I felt like everything that was happening was my fault, that I had caused all the discord within me and around me. I felt like a complete failure.

The culture I grew up in was never one to nurture differences. With segregation an unspoken agreement, it was easy to see that the world still hadn't evolved. It always confused me how on the playground in elementary school everyone played together, but by the time we reached junior high school there was a white section and a black section of the schoolyard. You can't talk about race in the South, even though its separation is apparent in our neighborhoods, our churches, and our schools. It's taboo to be different...even to be a white Southern girl who doesn't wear dresses isn't okay. Show up in a pair of pants to a bridal shower and talk about being ignored or glazed over. We still have real problems when it comes to a lot of things, and communicating about those problems is nearly impossible —it's much more convenient to sweep them under the rug.

Luckily, my parents had taught us to love everyone no matter what, so I knew there was hope and that deep down, perhaps, they would come around. All I had ever experienced was my parents accepting people from all walks of life and never hesitating to invite anyone from anywhere into our home. Maybe that was the downfall of it all —when it was their own daughter who was the one who was different, they couldn't stand on that loving foundation anymore because the fear was too big for them to see over. It seemed like I made it too hard for them to see me anymore. They couldn't see that loving, responsible, caring person behind my new label —they couldn't see her, and I was beginning to not see her either. I still knew her, but deep down she was lost and hurt. The world that I wanted to know and that I thought I knew had only existed in my mind, and that crushed me to pieces. I didn't know how to cope with feeling like I had lost everything, and I certainly didn't know how to fathom the feeling of saying goodbye to everything I knew.

I was used to proving myself. I was typically the only white girl who could really play basketball. Boys from our neighborhood would always challenge me to a game, and they would always go home embarrassed. I was really good at basketball, and I loved it. It gave me an opportunity to see that I was strong and confident. When I had traveled to play in most public high schools in Mississippi, I had pretty much always been the only white girl on the floor. I had had to prove myself over and over in order to find some sort of acceptance in the gym on any given night. I had always been up for the task and played my heart out. So I knew early on how to fight for acceptance, and I knew that I could get it if I worked hard enough and if I was confident enough.

When I came out of the closet, though, no matter how hard I worked, it was hard to see and even harder to feel if I was actually being accepted. It goes to show you that at the end of the day when we lay our heads on our pillows at night, we are only with ourselves and we only have ourselves to listen to and answer to. At this point, shooting baskets until the sun went down wasn't going to make the next day any better than the day before. The only option I had was to survive my brokenness, and the almost ten years since then have been about repairing my own self-confidence so I could climb back up and find out what I am truly made of.

There are many different moments in life when you feel trapped by failure. After I came out of the closet, that is all I felt...like a failure. I felt like I had thrown myself in the garbage and let everyone throw their trash on top of me. It wasn't easy trying to survive, trying to regain some sort of social acceptance that was fitting in everyone else's eyes.

I don't tell my sob story so that I can dwell in victimhood, I share it in order to share with you how I have been able to move from being a victim and seeing the world as against me to living an empowered life and knowing the world is for me. My story is the only one I truly know, it is the only one I can share and understand, so I share it in hopes that I will find even more healing and be able to better serve the world.

I never thought that I would be okay with being gay, and I also never thought that I would consciously choose to return here, to my home, Mississippi. I left pretty hastily after my older brother said to me, "You don't need to live here anymore. This place is not safe for you and you will be happier if you move." That pretty much summed up how I felt anyway, after the whole coming-out process. Seven years later, when I envisioned moving back to the Mississippi I had fled from, I cried. I cried because I was afraid. I was afraid because I knew it was going to challenge me and push me, even though I knew deep down that great things were in store for me. I thought I knew exactly what I would be doing once I got here, but I was both wrong and humbled along the way.

I remember standing in front of my friend's kitchen window in Fort Collins, Colorado, the day I got the vision to return home. My immediate reaction was to resist. After being gone for many years, after escaping the origin of my limited self-perception, was I really being asked to come back? Talk about pissed. No, talk about terrified. It was one of those moments in life that you can't brush off or forget the vision existed even if for a brief instant. When clarity is that clear, it lasts in your heart forever, and until I gave in it would have continued to push me its way.

I resisted at first, naturally, because the fear was too tall for me to see over. Even though I was already traveling back and forth between Colorado and Mississippi with my non-profit work, traveling to the South was one thing — living there was another. I wasn't ready to live there again, but something bigger than me knew I was preparing to fully step into my own healing. I cried tears of confusion, but behind all of my doubts, there was a knowing that trumped all my hesitation. I drove into the mountains of Colorado, asking and screaming, "Why now?! I don't want to go!!" But sitting on the rocks of disbelief near the water of opportunity, the mountains surrounded me with hope and faith and whispered to me, "You are stronger than you think." I think we are always stronger than we think, and I knew that the question of "why" wouldn't get an answer so quickly; nothing ever really gets answered when you choose a route that scares you.

The landscape of acceptance for people who are gay in Mississippi isn't exactly promising, but what I have since come to learn is that the opportunities to really find a way to love who you are abound. Moving back to Mississippi was a route I knew I had to choose, with all of the reasons I couldn't look ahead at and say, "Oh yeah, that makes perfect sense." This decision made me realize that there is a deep part of me that desired my return to Mississippi to find myself, and that I had to go...I had to go, and there was no negotiation because nothing else made sense anymore.

Life in Colorado was perfect. The mountains were beautiful, my friends were completely accepting of me, and my career was taking shape, but my soul was calling me "home" to Mississippi. I wasn't sure if my family wanted me back. Would they really be okay with having their openly gay family member come back to our small town? It was one thing to have a gay sister/daughter in another state, but in the same town again? Would I be shunned all over again? All my old fears re-surfaced, fears I had buried deep inside myself in an attempt to kill them. But I dug past their screams to the stillness of my soul and took the leap —into my fear and my own longed-for healing.

Over the last ten years, including the time since moving back to Mississippi, I have been rebuilding my confidence, and I'm finally scratching the surface of who I really am, deep down. The significance of this turning point in life for each of us is great. This is a time when you are truly coming to know who you want to be in the world, and if you choose who you know you are, you will have to dig deep enough to be able to rise above the perceptions you feel are against you. It takes courage to be who you are, and we all have that courage, but we all don't have to choose it.

This book has been an exercise in courage. I never thought I would have the guts to write it, because I knew it would expose parts of me that I would then need to look at, heal, and love. In fact, several years ago, I thought I would be writing a book with the title, "Everyone's Gay!" —talking about different types of discrimination, etc. That sounds courageous, especially when you're from Mississippi, but this book is different—it is me exposing myself on all levels. Up until now, I have had a widely read blog going, and each time I publish a new blog I get this sense of fear. I get scared because I know I am putting my heart out there, and that at any moment someone could trample all over my words and mistake me for someone I am not. I ask myself every time I publish a new blog, "Am I strong enough to handle any response with love?"

Luckily, I know myself enough that clicking that "Publish Live" button sends me into a greater sense of freedom than I had had moments before. And I know that I am strong enough to handle whatever comes my way. We all are.

We all go through tough and trying times that make us question who we are and choose who we want to be. Letting go of resentment and finding a way to love those I perceive as not loving me has been the driving force behind my own healing. Treating others the way you want to be treated has become cliché to most, but to truly embrace it and live it is no easy task because it requires you to look within and transform yourself. The only way back to remembering who you were when you entered this earth is to not only love those you feel rejected by or misunderstood by, but to embrace them.

The foundation of who I was and who I am has not changed over the years, but it has deepened. Transformation happens on a lot of different levels, but the depth of who you are never really disappears. I have learned that even when I am in the deepest pain, I can access the bigger part of me and have faith that the bigger part of me will pull me forward and eventually I will feel peace again.

The journey is far from over for me, but I have finally found a way back to me, back to the part of me that knows all is well. It also doesn't mean that I don't have down moments, or even down days, it just means that my faith in life is more complete and my confidence in myself has risen. All is well not because it is perfect but because I know that who I am is important, that I have a purpose to serve, and that I can truly get through anything.

My journey has been mostly about rising above others' perceptions. Rising above others' perceptions is not about getting to a place where you now look down on those you feel are against you, it is about getting to a place where you see those people as equals, realizing that your differences are just differences. Healing and forgiveness are processes that look different for everyone, and they are possible by getting in touch with who you want to be and then making choices that are in alignment with that —and eventually, you realize you were that person all along.

I first really told my story when I was interviewed by NPR, after moving back to Mississippi. I talked about how discrimination affected me as a gay woman who had grown up in Mississippi, how I dealt with and deal with it, and the kind of person I want to be. I was so nervous that I cried before the interview, and even more nervous before it aired.

I think I was afraid to tell my story and afraid to share my heart because when we expose ourselves — our pain, our joys, our lives — we run the risk of feeling unaccepted by others, only to realize that we actually aren't accepting ourselves. When we are brave enough to show who we are, we invite ourselves into life —life beyond our story, life beyond our feeling of being a victim. When we speak out or become more of who we are, then we welcome a light to shine around us and fear comes and goes...comes and goes.

I believe we are meant to be cooperative, loving people, each and every one of us, and I have always believed in the good in all people. The first step in becoming who we are all meant to be is being okay with who we are, and that takes tremendous courage. The more I hear life stories, the more I open up to our differences and feel even more connected to the complexity of our divine nature.

Just as all the drops of water make up the ocean, we as individuals make up what I like to call The U (Universe/God). If we are all a part of The U together, then surely your story is worth telling, and surely there is more for you beyond your story. "What was said to the rose that made it open, was said to me here in my chest" (Rumi).

It hasn't been easy being me. I don't think it is easy to be anyone. We all start out excited about life until we begin to embrace our personality, our individuality, and open our eyes to the fact that we don't want just the regular life that has been handed to us. We want an extraordinary life that is full of joy and happiness. But most of us don't want to do what it takes to have an extraordinary life because it is too scary or too impossible and may drive us to deal with our own pain (yikes!). And honestly, we don't want to be vulnerable – vulnerability takes commitment (daily commitment at that), forgiveness, and a lot of courage to move through tough times.

Ironically, though, it is in the very act of being vulnerable that we find our deeper courage. I know now that that courage is inside of me, and if it is in me then it must be in all of us.

CHAPTER 2

Agreeing To Disagree Is Not Enough

Agreeing to disagree is not enough. It just keeps us where we are.

—*Meagan O'Nan*

I used to be homophobic. Maybe things that are new to us human beings scare us, and so we react in ways that keep us from completely opening our hearts. Because if we open our hearts too much, we run the risk that someone else might not accept us if we embrace something too different, and then we will get hurt.

The first time I was exposed to a person who was gay (that I know of, anyway) wasn't until I was an upperclassman in high school. I knew on some level that I was different, but I only knew how to go through the motions of who I thought I wanted to be or should be. All a part of the process, I guess. Once I was around a few people who were gay in high school and college, I found myself saying, "Love the sinner, hate the sin." I would hang out with my gay friends quite a bit, but always hesitantly: what would my other friends/people think of me? Would they think I was gay too? A bit of foreshadowing, but isn't the game of life just that? Foreshadowing.

I remember sitting at my house about 12 years ago, listening to a friend of mine tell me that she was struggling with dating a woman because she didn't know if it was right or wrong. She couldn't find peace in her heart about it, so she was confiding in me. At the time, I was dating a guy and identified as straight (actually, I didn't identify as anything — as far as I was concerned, there only was "straight" — anything else was "wrong"), and my response and my feelings then were, "I love you, but I don't agree with being gay." That was my honest opinion. I truly loved my friend and I thought the most loving response was exactly what I said to her.

I think back to that day at my house with my friend and realize that what she needed from me was something much more—just a simple, "I love you. Follow your heart." That's what I needed too, and that's what I still need. It's what we all desire from those we love—to be seen, to be heard, to feel supported, and to feel uplifted. I choose to surround myself now with people who say these very things.

I admit that I often look back on that time in my life and feel regret for saying to my gay friends, "I love you, but I don't agree with your choice." I said it because that's what I knew and because I was scared of opening up to the fact that maybe love runs deeper than what I thought —deeper than what I had been exposed to. Who am I to tell someone else what their "sin" is? And what the heck, who are we to tell anyone if their choice is or isn't okay?

I didn't see it then, but in loving them and not agreeing with their "choice," I was putting qualifiers around my love and judging their choice as not okay. Love sees only love. Love is always supportive, respectful, accepting, honest, and willing. It doesn't use qualifiers like "but." So I wasn't really loving them, at least not in the way I see love.

Life loves irony, and it jumps at a chance to play it. When I realized I was gay about three years later, guess what I heard from others? "Meagan, I love you, but I don't agree with your choice." Or, "Meagan, I love you, but I hate your sin." I realized then that their "loving" response only served to underline the judgment that I was a sinner, or that I was wrong for being gay. As a result, I quickly embraced the feeling (and worse, the belief) of being less than and thought that this is what I deserved — I also felt I had to embrace it in order to get by. The tables had turned, and therein lies one of the greatest gifts of life: we do and say things that are eventually done unto us — and the gift is that we are given the opportunity to forgive the judgment and then forgive ourselves.

We forgive ourselves last because it is the hardest to do. When we hurt someone else, we have gone against our natural state (which is to love unconditionally), and so to deal with that pain we bury our regret and shame. Often, it takes someone else saying something equally as judgmental to pull that regret and shame out of us in order for us to see that ultimately it is ourselves that we are needing to forgive. Because this is a hard thing to do, we often point the finger and retaliate instead, continuing the cycle until one day suddenly our bodies are suffering, our heart is aching, we are feeling empty, and we finally realize that only we have the power to accept and love who we are....

It doesn't matter what scares you about someone, their pink hair, their tattoos, their piercings, maybe they are too skinny, or you think they are overweight — it just doesn't matter. Maybe you are a Christian and think New Agers are "out there" — or maybe you are a New Ager and think Christians need to "see the light and wake up!" The truth is, whatever scares you about someone else is an invitation to get to know who they are and to learn more about who you are — to give yourself an opportunity to break down a wall you have built against love over the years. And no, I am not saying that if you learn to fully accept a gay person then you will become gay — I am just saying that love is bigger than what we see or what we think we know.

We all change. Better said, we can all change. Eventually, as you accept more and love more, one day you will look in the mirror and love whom you see. But to get there, you have to give people an opportunity to love you — and give yourself the opportunity to love those who are different than you.

Life doesn't stop. There will always be tough times to remind us to crawl back into ourselves and feel the power of our own swat and who we are aiming at. I know that when I aim outward (if I am lucky enough to catch myself) then there is something to remember inward. I prefer to avoid these moments now, when I eventually end up here, writing it out, getting it out — figuring it out. I have had a lot of experiences in my life, and I realize there are a lot of things I don't know and may never know about life. But one thing is sure: Life is always speaking to me, trying to guide me in the direction that I requested the day before. There will always be fear. Fear is a part of life. What if I am not successful? What if someone asks me something and I don't know the answer? What if I "fail" again? I mean, a good life coach would know everything there is to know about life, right? Just like a good hair day sneaks up on me here and there, so do my fears. Sometimes it doesn't matter if I am doing all of the right things to take care of myself–they just pop up. Maybe fear days are good days, in the end, not bad ones —they are what push us to grow, if we treat them right. I am finding that giving my fears a good ole bear hug is much easier than acting like they don't exist. A real hug requires a giver and a receiver. Giving a hug is easy; receiving it —well, that is another story. Receiving fear sounds odd, but The U usually helps us out if we're open to it. Silly things will happen to me that nudge my perception from feeling attacked to suddenly feeling ridiculous that I ever felt attacked. Then I can ease away from the fake world I created in my head and at least acknowledge that I am scared of something. What that is, well, that is all a part of the ironic side of life.

When I acknowledge my fears, my humility returns, and I remember that no honest person would ever claim to know everything–in fact, most of the time, I realize I know nothing at all. That might be silly to admit, but life can and will surprise you in odd ways that no amount of effort to control it otherwise will change. I certainly don't want to act like I know how God will show up when I am brought all those things I request on a daily basis —peace, humility, understanding, joy, to name a few. Sometimes they come wrapped with a pretty bow, and other times the knock on the door is loud, annoying and painful, like when fears appear and the past is suddenly a part of your senses, nagging at you to indulge, take a bite and stay for a while. When I want to run away and scream my hurts onto the world, I remember that how I respond to life is what molds the days to come. So I sit down with Humility and write...or lash out at annoying bugs. Either way, I am committed to moving through my fears so that I can experience just how green the grass is on the other side. Otherwise, I will never really know how much deeper love can be or how vibrant the moment might appear.

Everything is always brighter after I let go. I tell myself to let go until I do. "Let go, Meagan, let go of it all." But what if all of these people who love and accept me decide not to, later? Ah yes, the truth —I might be rejected or told that I am not good enough anymore. But truth is truth —yes, I might be rejected, and so I must let it go, let it go, until that feeling is gone.

It's a reasonable fear, with years of rejection for being gay clouding my memory, but it's unreasonable now, in this moment. It feels like it would be nice to hold on tight to something that has been such a part of me — it served me well for a while, after all. It allowed me to protect myself, build a few walls and gather some experiences that have taught me who

I am and who I can be. But there comes a time when the best thing to do is throw yourself a rope and begin to climb to a place where your confidence is waiting for you, leaving the comfort of your fears behind. I asked for confidence yesterday, after all, and here The U is, uncomfortably offering me just what I asked for. If I don't jump into my fears with two feet, I will never know where I can stand without them.

Agreeing to disagree can be painful when you're on the receiving end of the "love." I have to admit, even today when someone says, "Meagan, I love you, but I disagree with your lifestyle choice," it stings. The sting isn't as deep as it used to be — it's a quick prick, and then it moves on. I know that don Miguel Ruiz says not to take things personally, but my wound hasn't sealed up completely yet, and I am not sure if it ever will. I have been working on it, and I have come a long, long way, but when you are told over and over that you are wrong for being who you are, or wrong for the choice you have made, it's easy to shut off to survive. And that's what I did: I stored the pain until I could deal with it. I'm still working through it, in layers. But just when I think I am over it, it surprises me again.

In saying all of this, I am not saying that to tell someone you disagree with them is wrong. I am saying that if it's said in the context of a "but," it hurts. When I hear, "I love you but," or "I love you even if," what goes in is the "but" and the "even if" — and the judgment it implies. I may believe and know I'm a good person at heart, but centuries of cultural shaming and condemnation and conditioning contribute to the hurt that follows an "I love you but." And as much as I would like to be strong enough to say it doesn't hurt, I would be lying. I'm not there yet. My dad always told me that I was going to have to have thick skin, but the thicker the skin, the more closed off my heart becomes. I don't want to live with a closed heart.

Agreeing to disagree is not enough. It just keeps us where we are.

"I love you even if you're gay."

"I love you even though you're married to a white/black/Asian person."

"I love you even though you converted to Catholicism/Judaism/Southern Baptist."

"I love you even though you live on the wrong side of the tracks."

"I love you even though you got pregnant before you got married."

Agreeing to disagree is not enough. It sends a message that one is better than the other — or at least, that's how I feel when I hear it. I believe we have to do better for our fellow people than agree to disagree, by encouraging them to be who they are, to be who they want to be, to be who they feel called to be, and to follow their heart on their journey. If we do that, then equality will happen naturally.

The above is from a blog that I wrote in March 2013. After I wrote this blog I got a lot of responses of support, ongoing dialogue, and personal attacks. Somehow, it brought about the conversation of whether being gay is right or wrong. This, of course, highlighted the very point I was trying to make —that in agreeing to disagree we make something right or wrong and that *that* is the issue. But the whole dynamic of agreeing to disagree is so subtle that we often get sucked into it without even realizing — and in this instance, I wasn't immune either.

One person in particular, "Jane," was especially vicious with her comments, questioning me, calling me names, and saying things that were (in my opinion at the time) "wrong." I disagreed with her enough that I began to not only delete some of her posts, I even began to delete them before reading them because I assumed they would be more of the same. Ultimately, I blocked her from commenting at all. Here is one of Jane's comments:

> "The person who loves Meagan will warn her against abiding in her sin, because the Bible is clear

that homosexuals will not inherit the Kingdom of God (1 Cor. 6:9-11). The person who loves Meagan will think of Meagan and not themselves as they care more for her eternal life than the approval of Meagan. The person who loves Meagan simply must encourage and help her through the hard time of repentance."

The comments continued to get worse as others were taking up for me, which led me to delete post after post. I was doing this to protect myself, but I also wanted to be "fair" to Jane, so I asked others (who were being supportive of me and challenging Jane) to re-submit their authentic comments to make my blog "right" in the way I wanted to see it—without any "stones thrown."

And therein lies the irony: I did to Jane, and to those defending me, what had been done to me. I made them "wrong" with my own actions, despite my good intentions, when I know deep inside that there is a place for us all to reside, a place where there is no right and no wrong. I was judging and putting qualifiers on my ability to love. I wrote a followup blog with the following:

To Jane, I am sorry that I lost my way—I am sorry if I made you feel insignificant by not allowing you to post freely—and I am sorry to everyone who I asked to reconsider posting a certain way in the name of right and wrong. I know that I am only responsible for me and that beyond that any attempt to control leads to confusion, misplaced judgment, and a need to run further from what is true for me.

Although most of you agreed with how I handled the situation, deep down in me something was stirring that didn't feel right. I got caught up in the need to control just as I have over the years... "You are not good enough, you don't deserve equal rights, you are second class." Even if no one said those things directly to me, that's what I heard, and in an effort to protect myself I sought control.

As hard as I have tried to rise into my higher self, I still feel a need to protect—and control. I am not attempting to be either a martyr or a masochist, I simply realize that I have no right to tell anyone if they are right or wrong, or for God's sakes, if their comments are good enough for my blog.

I read an article this morning on the new pope and how he recently went to wash and kiss the feet of prisoners. In our society today, prisoners are not perceived as human beings but as lost souls who have no hope—they are cast aside—and yet there the pope went to demonstrate that their worthiness is equal to everyone else's. We learn early on in traditional Christianity that we are not worthy, that we "don't deserve." But I have come to see differently...I believe we are worthy of all of the wonderful things in our lives. It is that very belief of unworthiness that has stifled me in the past to think that I deserve hardship without experiencing any joy within it. And that just doesn't feel like truth to me.

I know deep down that beyond what is "right" and what is "wrong" there is a part of me that connects me to everyone—even to those who discredit me the most. To deny anyone the right to speak their own truth and to represent themselves however they so choose to is to ultimately deny myself. When I deny myself...then I suffer. Aren't I trying to embody and present the message that we all deserve full opportunities to be who we are? Yes.

If there were concrete "rights" and "wrongs" that felt good and true to us all, then I believe we would all abide by them—but there are not, so we

battle along the way instead of just listening to
what's inside. Even in the name of war we make
it "okay" to murder—calling it killing instead of
murdering.

That's why I feel I must listen to the deepest
part of me to find what is true for me, and act accordingly. I am truly sorry, Jane, for neglecting you. I
realize that my action discredited you. I also want to
thank you for healing something inside of me—you
gave me an opportunity to see myself in you, and
that has brought me a lot of freedom. My heart feels
lighter and my chest more expansive than before.
I know now that when I trust the power of my own
inner truth I don't need to defend myself...

Truth is never exhausting or complicated,
and when we encounter it, there is no big emotion
attached to it, either—just peace.

When we look at the controversy over whether
being gay is right or wrong, or whether it is a sin or
not a sin, it is only a controversy because everyone
is searching for the answer. But maybe there is no
answer and nothing to search for except the knowing that your personal choices that feel in alignment

with who you are, are what will ultimately bring you the peace we all feel drawn to.

Looking back, Jane's words reminded me of old wounds, and at the time I couldn't handle them. But now I see that because of her words I was able to heal in a way that I don't think I even understand yet, and may never come to understand. I do know, though, that Jane is just as worthy as anyone else, and so am I."

This experience is a good example of how, when another's words hurt us, we are quick to respond in ways that don't respect the other person, as I did in this case. And that's exactly the point —we respond in those ways when we are confronted with something that makes us uncomfortable, whether that is a person who is gay or a person who has an issue with someone being gay. Jane was uncomfortable with my being gay, and she responded hurtfully, and I was uncomfortable with her "attack," and so I responded in a way that didn't respect her, and in the end that ultimately hurt me.

All of this has given me a deep awareness of how words hurt, no matter how well intended they may be, and so I try to always choose them carefully. Life is hard enough as it is, and I truly try to live in a way that gives people hope and belief in themselves and their choices, even when I am feeling down, insecure, and confused —and especially when I think I may be right. Everyone has a story. I often think that my life would have been easier if I had just married a man, had kids, and gotten a regular job. I could have chosen that (not that I think being gay is a choice —"being" married to a man is an action —it doesn't change who you are). But those thoughts are fleeting–they go as quickly as they come. Plus, when my partner enters a room, my heart experiences joy, a smile crosses my face, and my world feels lighter. I remember very quickly why my heart led me here, why the turmoil was necessary, and that I deserve every bit of that joy that floods my heart. So, even though there is a part of me that still questions, a part of me that might still believe I am less than (transforming beliefs takes time), I pray for a better time when we will all feel welcome in this world, and I push myself and try to absorb those moments when the details that separate us don't seem so important.

Everyone has experienced pain, and everyone (hopefully) has experienced love. Everyone has insecurities and fears. I don't know the history behind the face I see, I only know my own, and so I strive to be as responsible as I can with each word I choose to express so that what I put out there is what I would wish back. I may not always express love to my fullest capability, but it is my wish each day that I do the best I

can — that I leave an imprint on someone's heart that needed
a lift. Agreeing to disagree blocks us from honoring another's
story and attaches us to "right" and "wrong," and in the process
people get hurt and hearts close in defense. When we hear, "I
love you but," we close off. When we hear, through words or
actions, "I love you," our hearts burst open. In the last three
years that Clare and I have lived in Mississippi, every time we
get an invitation with my name next to Clare's my heart leaps
with joy. I feel seen. I feel supported. I feel loved. Something
so small — but something needed, something that says, "You're
welcome here." Even if the person inviting us disagrees with
our "lifestyle," they are willing to put themselves in a position
to be uncomfortable, and I admire that. A step is a step closer,
and I must be more willing to show up to parties and be more
present instead of preparing for someone to say something
that could make me feel less than.

I know that an open heart leads to depth and connection,
and depth and connection lead to change. I want to be a part
of the change, so I too have to be willing — to be honest when I
am hurt, but still willing — to let love in.

Just this past December, my dad's mother passed away.
When I had visited with her the October before, she had told
me that she was ready, so I knew it wouldn't be long. My dad
has seven brothers and sisters, and all 70 of us extended

family were at the funeral except Clare. Clare's daughter was coming in from Seattle the same day as the visitation, and a snow/ice storm had flooded the area, so she and her daughter couldn't make the drive to Northern Kentucky in our Chevy Cruze. Plus, she had a horrible cold – in other words, all odds were against her. She still tried, though, frustrated because she could see that it just wasn't meant to be. My family told her to not even try, and I agreed.

The funeral was beautiful. I remember feeling stuck in time as I looked over my family in the pews of the Catholic Church I had grown up in, and I could see my grandparents at the front of the church proudly looking over us, so proud of what they had created. I was proud too, proud to be a part of something so powerful. I couldn't contain my tears that day because the love I felt was so overwhelming. When I returned home from Kentucky, I felt so moved and so touched from that experience with my family.

Several days after the funeral, a cousin of mine called me and asked to speak to Clare. I was a bit confused by his request, but I handed her the phone, and when she hung up, with tears in her eyes she told me what he had said: "The family wasn't complete without you at the funeral."

Love can move a mountain of doubt inside another person. It can heal layers upon layers of hurt. My cousin, through that one act of love, was able to help me heal any doubt or questions I had had about all 70 people seeing Clare and me as equals. There was no "but" in that "I love you."

At some point, we all have to ask ourselves, "What kind of person do I want to be for others?" My cousin changed my life in that moment, simply by reaching out and stretching his heart to embrace us and make us feel a part of the family. My guess is he was just doing what came naturally to him, what on my end felt like the biggest dose of validation that I could have needed.

Courage comes when hearts are willing to be hurt, and unconditional love is what helps us heal. My heart is open again because I found the courage to dive into my fears, embrace them, and love who I am. Where there used to be insecurity and perceived condemnation, I now choose to love myself, and every day I want to make the choice to love others in the way I want to be loved.

One of my favorite quotes comes from the great Persian mystic, Rumi: "Out beyond ideas of wrongdoing and right-doing, there is a field, I will meet you there." The poem continues: "When the soul lies down in that grass, the world is too full to talk about. Ideas, language, even the phrase 'each other' doesn't make any sense."

One day, I hope, we'll all be there.

CHAPTER 3

Transforming Our Pain Into Love

I learned that courage was not the absence of fear, but the triumph over it. The brave man is not he who does not feel afraid, but he who conquers that fear.

—*Nelson Mandela*

I remember being ganged up on by a group of girls when I was a young teenager. It was a sleepover and they all wanted one specific girl to fight me. It was clear that the girl they talked into fighting me didn't want to. I remember her hesitation, looking at them and saying "no" until they started yelling at her to do it and cheering her on. I waited in fear, and regardless of what she didn't want to do, she punched me as hard as she could in the chest. It hurt so bad, inside and out.

I, feeling helpless and completely alone, buried my pain quickly. I stood tall and with anger burning in my chest looked into the eyes of the girl who hit me. I got closer and closer to her, and when I got close enough to touch my nose to hers, in complete rage I picked her up over my head and slammed her on the pillows. Underneath the pillows was something hard, and in that moment I experienced both a horror at the thought that I had hurt her and a realization that hurting her wasn't what I really wanted; what I really wanted was for my pain to go away. (It turned out the pillow protected her from whatever it was that was hard; she was fine and I learned a valuable lesson.)

The wound that developed in me from this experience was deep. I still feel it. I believe the wound is deep because I have always believed in the goodness of others and have always tried my hardest to see that goodness, and in that experience neither her goodness nor mine came out. But, as with any wound, it is not important to know why it exists, only to feel its pain so that you can move on and remember the goodness in people again.

I think I have held onto this experience throughout my life, afraid on some level to become a part of a group that might turn on me at some point as this group did. This hasn't been a conscious fear but something that has resided inside me and replayed itself at different times in my life.

Now I understand that healing that wound is what will set me free from the cycle and help me to be more compassionate, understanding, and trusting.

> *"When I find myself reacting with anger or opposition to any person or circumstance, I will realize that I'm only struggling with myself. Putting up resistance is a response created by old hurts. When I relinquish this anger, I will be healing myself and cooperating with the flow of the universe."* —Deepak Chopra

Yeah, I fought back at that slumber party, but looking back on how I felt after fighting back, I realize that's not who I want to be now. Fighting back is much more exhausting than loving. Plus, as Deepak says in the above quote, anger is a resistance to dealing with old hurts — it creates new wounds and buries old ones deeper.

When we stuff pain, it inevitably surfaces. If we haven't dealt with the pain we have stuffed, we end up using that pain by putting it on others. One of the reasons that discrimination is so real in our society is because we all have wounds to heal. We come into this world believing in love, and then when we experience the opposite of what we perceive to be love, we build barriers to keep ourselves from feeling hurt any further.

What is so hard to learn is that the empowering thing to do is to love those who scare us so that we can believe again —but that takes a willingness to turn the doorknob slowly on a door that's often hidden in layers of your wall.

Call me crazy, but I don't believe that anyone truly hurts anyone else on purpose. Hurting others goes against our true nature. I believe that when we hurt others we are just acting out of a need to protect ourselves in the hopes that if we hurt, we won't get hurt. We lose touch with our true nature by looking outwards, but the best way to get that hope is to give it, and to give it requires a willingness to look inwards and be who you truly are, a loving human being. Turn your doorknob —I know I have been turning mine.

One of the chances I had to turn my doorknob happened shortly after I moved back to Mississippi. At the time, I was running a non-profit organization I had started, and because I wasn't taking home a paycheck for my work I was doing a lot of side jobs to get by (painting houses, caretaking, etc.). For one of the jobs that I would work occasionally, Clare would work with me as well. The owner of the company we were working for didn't know that we were a couple. At the time, we weren't as open; however, a friend of ours also worked for this company, and she, of course, knew we were partners. After working for this company off and on for several months, an opportunity for forgiveness arose.

The owner of the company somehow figured out that Clare and I were partners and got really scared about what others would think of him and his wife if they continued to allow us to work for them. He let my friend know that his wife was really unhappy about our involvement with the business. Because this company had ties with the school district, they were especially worried about how our working for them might appear to parents — their customers. In fact, the owner's wife went as far as to go into the school records to make sure I had passed my background check (my non-profit was working with the school district, so I was on file). Whether she actually checked my background check or not, I am not sure, but I will tell you that I even started questioning myself through this process. Would she find something on my background check that I didn't know about? How crazy is that? — I knew I was clear and that there was nothing at all in my history that could possibly keep me from working with children.

I was so angry and hurt throughout this process. Our friend let the owner know that she had told us everything that was going on (which in itself was a true act of courage). He knew that we were amazing workers and that we were really good with the kids we were working with, and for whatever reason, he told our friend he felt bad about his wife behaving the way she did. One morning shortly after all this, he showed up at our front door. I didn't want to see him, so I ran upstairs. Clare let him in. He came in and sat down. Clare came upstairs and forced me to come down. I was feeling scared, rejected, unsure, and really angry. But I went downstairs to give it a chance.

The owner sat there crying and apologizing, admitting that he had never been around a gay couple and that his wife was out of line for doing what she did. He admitted that he, too, was out of line for everything that he had done and said. While he was talking, I kept my arms folded in front of my chest as if to protect myself, and I kept quiet. The more he talked, though, I began to observe myself changing. I opened up my sitting stance a little, and I even began to speak up at some point. Eventually, I told him I forgave him but that I could not work for him any longer. It felt good to stand my ground a bit.

After that day, whenever we ran into him, I would start to get nervous —but I would never run away or avoid him. I always made a point to initiate a conversation to bridge the gap between my fear and the love I wanted to feel towards him. I would get butterflies in my stomach each time I ran into him, but I knew that if I avoided him I would be going against my own beliefs on how I believe we are to treat one another. The trick is to never run away. Face your fear. Have the courage to embrace those who scare you until they don't anymore. Eventually, the butterflies went away and there was no emotion when I saw him. But it took a lot of incidences of running into each other and a lot of action — and courage — on my part. Action is necessary when you are trying to transform your pain into love. There is no other way. I didn't want to embrace him, but something inside told me I had to if I wanted to become the person that I want to be. After every embrace, I felt more like myself than I would have by avoiding him.

We human beings build our existence on our egos to keep ourselves from being hurt, ashamed, or pushed to the side. We oppress others so that we ourselves won't feel oppressed. We spend our lives fighting to be on top — but when we get there, there is dissatisfaction unless we have been able to connect with the truth of who we are. Climbing on the backs of others, whether through manipulation or oppression, is never the truth of who we are.

Oppression can only exist as long as we allow it in our own lives. To break any pattern in our history means to stand up with great courage and commit to wanting to see the victim as the victor — as an equal. This is as true for individuals as it is for civilizations. The moment we think another is wrong in the way they live their life is the moment we become an oppressor ourselves. But with this belief comes great responsibility to take a good look in the mirror when we feel the urge to judge or look down upon another. Rather than putting all of our energy into changing another person, we start to realize that empowerment comes when we look within and give ourselves the opportunity to be more of who we actually want to be. I may have been justified on one level in my experience with my former "boss" by pointing the finger at him as the oppressor, but in so doing I made myself the oppressor too, and it was only in my willingness to sit with my discomfort and look in the mirror that I was able finally to break the pattern of oppression that we had both created.

As long as we remain committed and connected to our own purpose and personal journeys, we serve others by meeting them where they are with unconditional love. There is a challenge in living this way: it may mean that you will never be right in the eyes of others. But the reward is far greater when you discover that by embracing all of who you are the love you share with others is magnified tenfold.

Forgiveness is easier when you are able to step back and see that the only path you are responsible for is your own. Embracing your own hurt and pain is a part of the human process, and if you try to avoid it, you will hurt others. Transforming your hurt and pain into a deeper experience of love takes patience and courage —and faith that all will eventually unfold just as your heart has always envisioned. Being all of who you are and allowing yourself to flow with the ever-changing ways of life allows you a sense of freedom —a belief in the magnificence of your own inner world to a point where your outer world becomes a direct reflection.

'Soon after moving back to Mississippi, I was at a social event where I was given another opportunity to rise above my initial reaction. From across the room, I saw a preacher walk in who had given me a hard time years before when I had come out of the closet. This was the first time I had run into him since I had moved back; in fact, I had never anticipated running into him at all, but there he was. I knew that I could avoid him the entire event because there were enough people there to make that possible, and for a brief moment I considered doing just that. But deep down I also knew that if I were to avoid him I would also be avoiding a wonderful opportunity for my own healing. So, once I knew what I had to do, I didn't waste any time. I walked across the room before I could change my mind and said, "Hey, do you remember me?" He was shocked that I even approached him, and he seemed really uncomfortable. I reached out and gave him a hug, and he hugged me back. I asked him a few questions about his life, and we had a very brief conversation. Since then, I have run into him many more times, and I can now approach him without hesitation or nervousness. The first time is always the hardest, but time heals all.

We don't always have to have tough conversations to heal. Sometimes, as in the example above, it's just a simple mutually respectful interaction that sets the tone for who you know you want to be. Most of the time, it has to be you who initiates the interaction, and you may have to choose to be yourself even while the other person is struggling to do so. But that is also where you will find your reward —by choosing to be who you want to be. And each time you choose to be who you want to be, you are able to let go of old hurts and transform a little bit more of your pain into love.

Healing isn't easy work; it requires you to act in a way that sometimes takes all the courage you have. Remember, though, that when you are given an opportunity to rise into your courage and act on something that scares you, you have been prepped for that very moment. Courage doesn't exist without fear; the very experience of being scared is itself a call for courage.

The U doesn't make mistakes, so when you are presented with a chance to build yourself up and build others up, take it. When you see someone in the grocery store that you want to avoid, don't go down other aisles in an attempt to avoid a potentially uncomfortable conversation. In avoiding it, you are only running away from yourself. It doesn't ever feel good to run away, and you will be the one who suffers. When you feel fear, be the first to hug or say hi to the person who is evoking that fear inside of you. Not only will your experience be better, but your soul will appreciate your taking the time to honor its true nature. And who knows? You might just make their day.

We human beings have such a long history of oppression and repression, and it can only shift a moment at a time — in each moment where we see ourselves as an equal to all others, and all others as equal to us. To rise above means to embrace all that you truly are, and to see everyone else as their own person. If you rise too high so that you look down on another, then life is likely to humble you so that you remember who you are — not above others and not below. Viewing life this way constantly challenges us to deepen our relationship with our fears, but it also encourages us to understand that on the other side of our fears is a greater experience that we all seek, that of our true nature, that of love.

CHAPTER 4

Being Who We Really Are

"It takes courage to grow up and become who you really are."

— *E.E. Cummings*

Since I was a little girl, I have practiced speeches about unity and love in the shower. I have pretended over and over that I am in front of thousands of people speaking about the truth of who we really are. I still practice. I often envision what I would do if I were speaking at an event and someone screamed words of discrimination at me, or if someone asked a question in an unloving way. I always imagine that my response would be so loving and so open that any negative discord in the air would be transformed and all of our lives would be changed.

I picture it all the time—what I would do in tough situations. The part of me doing the envisioning is the part of me that knows what is real about who we are —the part of me that I ignore when I'm in a crowded room, as I often let my voice shy away from doing what I know I want to do. But I'm slowly but surely climbing out of my shell, learning to listen to my inner callings, remembering my envisioned scenarios and starting to take action much quicker. I'm certain the courage it takes to do this comes from a place of knowing who I am rather than just presenting the person I think people will accept. It's a tough battle but a common one for us all.

One of the most profound things anyone ever said to me was, "There is nothing wrong with you. You are perfect the way you are." At the time, I was struggling to make sense of life and felt like everything was wrong with me, and so the timing of this statement was profound. A simple statement like this may seem like common knowledge to many, but knowing something and actually embracing it are two totally different things. If there is ever anything I can give to anyone during my time on this earth, it is what this statement gave to me: There is nothing wrong with you. You are perfect the way you are.

When I talk about being perfect the way you are, I mean who you *really* are. Who we really are beyond the surface of our exterior world is a spirit, a soul waiting to express itself authentically. We spend so much of our lives trying to be who our parents think we should be and who society encourages us to become that we neglect our own inner calling and purpose and end up plagued with inner dissatisfaction. At that point, a choice, conscious or not, is made between unhappiness and joy. We either begin to make choices that highlight who we really are or continue making choices that take us down a path that outwardly appears easier but inwardly deadens us.

After experiencing so much pain as a result of my coming-out process, I figured out that the only way I could turn that pain into self-empowerment was to identify the part of me that knew truth on an intimate level —to become more familiar with that part of me and then learn to make choices that were in alignment with who that was. This hasn't happened overnight; it has required a continual willingness to sift through all my experiences and memories of defeat, struggle, sadness, and failure. Accessing the deeper, true part of who we are is always possible in every moment, but it requires us to be willing to take a good hard look at ourselves and the choices we've made in our lives.

Religion (Christianity, in my experience) has played a powerful part in my own self-defeat by telling me that I am a sinner and not worthy of God's love. When you are taught that you are imperfect and unworthy, then you begin to believe it — and when you believe it, you suffer. It is a self-fulfilling prophecy. Luckily, I knew deep down that I was not a sinner and that I *was* worthy; I somehow knew to question it because it didn't feel loving to me. But climbing through the abyss of doubt was no easy task, especially when all you had been taught reinforced it. Thankfully, I was exposed later to new ways of thinking that worked better for me, and I began to question everything that I had been taught about God and love. Things started to align for me, and I found others who believed what I knew was true in the way I felt — that God is love and that I am perfect.

Even though you know something, it doesn't always mean you're living it. My first book, "Creating Your Heaven on Earth," was written at a time when I was in the middle of a relationship that was taking a turn for the worse. Soon after signing my book contract with Dreamriver Press, I started to see that the relationship was headed in a bad direction and that I had to figure it out. It was painful, very painful — mostly because I had never been forced to look at myself in such a way that required me to love myself enough to leave. A couple of months into realizing that I wouldn't be able to have the life I wanted with this woman, she broke it off, and I am glad now that she did. Although my strength and belief in myself were increasing, my fear of change was still very much present.

Having her end the relationship was a huge gift for me, and it was at that point that I started to turn a corner for myself because it was the only way for me to move forward. We both wanted different things for our lives, and that is why the tension had grown and why we had both become foreigners in our own home. While the beginning of our relationship had been wonderful, it took a series of painful events to help push us forward into seeing that we were heading in different directions and that we had to let go.

This experience taught me so much — most of all that life gives you what you need when you need it. Somehow, I was able to write a self-help book when what I needed most was to help myself. And writing that book saved my life because it helped me see that I can access the bigger part of who I am regardless of the situation I am in. (Life's sense of humor also came through loud and clear in this experience: writing "Creating Your Heaven On Earth" was the very vehicle that brought me to my own heaven on earth, which is where I am on most days now.)

Who you really are never disappears. You either choose to see it or you don't. The longer you ignore the part of you that wants to be revealed in your external world, the more pain you will feel. Accessing your truth happens when you take the time to nurture yourself. When you take the time to connect to your higher self/God/Universe/Spirit, then you begin to see life differently and you begin to make choices that make more sense for who you are deep down.

There is something inside each of us that knows we are meant to live a life full of joy coupled with a deep sense of fulfillment. It doesn't mean that hard moments won't come your way, it simply means that there is a part of you that trusts life and all that unfolds with it. Accepting that life can and will be difficult for you at some point is half the battle. Once you know that life is going to be what life is going to be, then you start to see that the small and big choices you make in your everyday life are meaningful because they add up to who you are choosing to be in each moment. When you choose outside of what your heart desires, then life will give you opportunity after opportunity to get in tune with yourself again. If you don't listen to life's nudges, it will nudge you so hard until you do listen. The part of you that knows all is well has to be nourished so that you can go out in the world and make choices that reflect that part of you. Your own road to fulfillment is present in every moment you are given.

Beneath it all, who I am is who you are. Being who we really are is the task set before us throughout our lives, and it is a task worth paying attention to. Listening to your heart when you are making decisions may mean taking risks, and it may mean that you stick out, but the rewards within those risks are worth it. Who you really are is never lost…just listen for those inner callings that lead you back to the bigger part of who you are.

We humans have built our cultures around ourselves to protect us from being hurt by others. The name of the game here on earth is hurt, be hurt, heal, move on—again: hurt, be hurt, heal, move on. We all play a part in this game. We all have trust issues because we have all been hurt. Plus, you can't guarantee that you will never hurt another because you can't know all of the expectations they have built around who they want you to be for them. Life can become a very complicated game when we are constantly trying to protect ourselves from being hurt by other people. The most we can do in any moment is to be aware of who it is we want to be, and be that. When we come from a place of genuineness, we can trust our intentions and let the rest go. We all experience hurt, and we all experience resentment, and we all cause both in others. If we want to heal, we need to let them go.

In order to be willing to move past any resentment and fear you've been holding onto over the years, you must first acknowledge that they exist and then consider where they originated. Once you have done that, then you can become more open to letting them go. No one ever said that life was easy; in fact, working through resentment and fear means you must work through all the feelings of pain that are behind those resentments and fears. The tougher part of the process is the commitment you must then make to yourself to no longer make choices that stem from pain but rather from the light inside that is trying to help you. I have seen so many clients over the years who tell me that they have everything they ever wanted —the house, the car, the family, the job, etc. – and that they are still miserable. Even when you have everything you have ever wanted, it's tough to really appreciate it if you haven't taken the time to heal what needs to be healed. We are so good at stuffing our emotions and we are never really taught how to deal with them, so we go through life stuffing our pain and then end up putting it on others.

When I first came out of the closet, it was easy for me to slip into a victim mentality. Everyone was coming at me in disbelief that I was gay. People were trying to convince me that I was wrong and that I was going to hell, and there was a large part of me that believed them. Thankfully, there was another part of me that knew there was more to life than what I had been taught up until that point. I had a professor during that time who told me that she saw the Divine in me. Although I didn't quite understand what she meant at the time, the bigger part of me recognized the truth in what she said. That same spark she saw in me, is in everyone. From then on, my story became about digging through the layers and years, trying to grasp onto the parts of me that I knew were not broken. It took time to put all of the pieces together, but eventually I could actually see that I was never broken to begin with.

Trusting life is something I believe is inherent in each one of us, although finding that part of us isn't always easy. In order to move forward, I had to be willing to see that life was on my side. It has taken me a good ten years to get to a place of no longer wanting to self-destruct. I see now that I am the creator of my life and that when I feel stuck I have to ask the question, what do I need to let go of in this moment? We humans so often react without thinking, with the need to keep ourselves from getting hurt, that we forget to consider there may be a choice that would be better for us. As a result, we end up just trying to survive and miss out on actually living because we don't recognize that in each moment we are given a chance to heal.

A big part of being who we really are is re-discovered when we acknowledge our shame, face our fears and put ourselves out there. I recently put myself out there by blogging about my own fears around getting married:

The thought of getting married terrifies me. Not because I don't want to get married, it's just all of the fears that come with the thought of it. Will everyone truly want to be there and not feel weird about it? Will I feel awkward and uncomfortable? I know I am gay, but I am still sifting through whether I "deserve" a wedding day or not—and let's be honest, having a ceremony where it isn't legal and may not be for a while isn't that appealing (even though I definitely know that I would want it to be in Mississippi).

And the fears carry on: Am I ready to fully be me at such a ceremony? Will people be excited when I tell them I am getting married? Or will they have no response at all, or "okay" and "head nod" responses, or just be uncomfortable? Will I have to be careful who I invite because they may not "agree" with my choice to get married? Should there be a kiss at the ceremony? A hug? It feels like coming out again. Preparing for the worst, slightly hoping for the best, while still knowing deep down that incredible outcomes are possible .

The thought of telling my family and friends that I want to get married makes me sick to my stomach—I can't bear the thought of possibly going through what I have been through before... Deep down, when I think of telling others that I am getting married, I feel the need to beg, "Please support me. Please support me. Don't hurt me with your words or lack thereof. Don't tell me you don't agree but you'll support me anyway. Don't tell me you don't understand and that you won't come because your faith is more important to you. Don't do it. Please just support me and love me. Please just be excited and let's celebrate!"

As I have been evaluating my process, I am very aware of my fears while still holding onto the dream of having a ceremony of some sort. I realize a few things that are standing in my way that I am ready to let go of. Above the doorway to my dream is a sign that says, "Forgiveness." I may appear to be someone who is able to let go easily, but I am not. At the same time, I understand and trust that my process is unique to me and that it is necessary for it to be as it is. I acknowledge that I have held onto being looked down upon by the majority of our society. It is embedded so deeply even though things are in the midst of changing. I have allowed others' beliefs to seep into my own and have been yanking at the seams of breaking open and showing my full self.

A wedding would be that for me — a full expression of who I am. All of my vulnerability, every bit of my courage, every ounce of trust that I have, and my willingness to get hurt by fully putting myself out there to be looked upon, to be loved in a new way, and to ultimately accept myself. It will take all of me to do it, and it will take all of those around me. In order to welcome all to take part in my dream, I know I must forgive the past — the past that remains inside of me. And I will continue to forgive over and over and over — including forgiving myself for all of the times when I just couldn't muster up the courage to fully be who I am.

A big part of being who we really are is re-discovered when we acknowledge our shame, face our fears and put ourselves out there. Writing this blog helped me uncover further shame that I had around being gay, i.e., an underlying belief that I don't deserve to get married. By writing about my fears, I was able to let them go and then have a few great conversations with my family members. I can see now that my fears weren't unreasonable, but by expressing them I was able to move on. Putting yourself out there can be scary, but vulnerability has a way of transforming your pain into love so that you can get back to who you really are.

Who you really are never changes. Not too long ago, a professor of mine from graduate school at Mississippi State University sent me a PowerPoint that I had done for one of my classes in 2004. I had given a presentation to the class during which I had told them I was gay, and then I gave the PowerPoint, and this is what it said:

What Do You See

You see my smile...what do you see?

Do you look into my eyes or do you avoid them?

I say the things that I have always wanted to say and I am punished for a wrong that I did not commit.

My heart is put on hold because I let you get the best of what I truly represent.

You tell me to run away —

I cry, and yet, stand firm.

If my heart...my ways,

Aren't what you expected —

Aren't what you understand,

Then please cast me aside and make me an object of complete imperfection.

I seek what it is what you desire unchanged,

HAPPINESS;

And I am still just a woman lost because of your perception.

I am exhausted from trying to explain, and tired that I let you get the best of me.

But, today...TODAY, you will not faze me.

Today, I will get the best of you.

I force you to love me without saying a word because you will see that

I am ONLY a woman.

Only a woman, with a heart, with a mind,

And a WILL to overcome the blurred reality of convenience.

I AM A WOMAN

Who can speak for myself

Who can stand alone without you.

I have my God, I have my heart...that's all I need.

I WILL LOVE YOU ANYWAY.

On reading through the presentation, I remembered that day. I had been so scared to share myself with my class. It had also been during a time that was extremely hard for both me and my family, and so I was feeling really alone. On top of that, I was being questioned and treated unfairly by so many. So when I read this presentation nine years later, I was surprised to be able to recall how brave I had been and how strong I was. Yes, me, I was so strong! It brings tears to my eyes when I think about it.

What it took for me to do that then—to be so raw, so vulnerable, to just lay it on the line —is what it still takes for me in many situations today. I remember after that class all I got was support and encouragement from my classmates, but I believe that was so because I was able to be so open and vulnerable. It is in those states of vulnerability that I believe we can really see each other.

In this experience of remembering back, I was also astounded to see that even then all I craved was to find a way to love those who were giving me a hard time. In fact, around the time that I gave this presentation, I remember a couple of people from the Fellowship of Christian Athletes had come to me and asked me to meet them at the chapel on campus to have a conversation. They had shown up and told me that I was going to go to hell if I remained in my "immoral lifestyle." They had read passage after passage to me, describing what hell would be like if I continued to choose to live "the gay lifestyle." A part me had wanted to get up and run away, but instead I just lied and said I was no longer in a relationship with a woman so that we could pray and get on with the day.

Since then, I have worked on finding a way to love those who reject me. I have been very frustrated by the process because it has taken time, a lot of courage, a lot of doubt, and a lot of getting up after falling on my face. When I doubt who I am in the world and the difference I am making, I can think back to this moment in my life (this presentation and PowerPoint) and remember that even in the midst of so much pain my soul knew where it wanted to go – to find a way to love those who don't see me. Behind it all, I know that the process of loving others is all about loving and accepting myself – and that takes time, patience, and a willingness to remain vulnerable and open.

Our prime purpose in this life is to help others. And if you can't help them, at least don't hurt them.

—The Dalai Lama

CHAPTER 5

Going Back To Your Roots: Healing Through Tough Conversations

Courage is what it takes to stand up and speak;
courage is also what it takes to sit down and listen.

—*Winston Churchill*

We all want our family members to love and accept us for who we really are, which often results in strange dynamics having to do with roles, expectations, and past hurts. What we often fail to realize, though, is that these dynamics don't happen because we don't love one another but rather because we do.

We all spend so much energy in life around this deep desire to want our family members to love and accept who we are, but what we are really seeking is something that neither they nor anyone else can give us — our own full love and acceptance of ourselves.

I hear so many stories from people who are being discriminated against by their families. The pain that results from this runs deep because home is the one place where you want to be loved and accepted the most. Discrimination and rejection by families can happen on many issues: coming out as a gay person; wanting to practice a different religion or way of life; entering into a bi-racial relationship; wanting to travel the world and not have a "real" job — or wanting the "security" of a real job and not understanding wanting to travel the world. We are who we are.

Family ties — whether healthy or not — are most often the deepest because our family is the "tribe" we are born into. If we feel as though we have been denied by our family — whether it be everyone in the family or just one family member — then we feel that life has denied us in some way and we feel completely alone and unsure.

On my own journey, it has taken time and a lot of painful introspective work, but this is what I have discovered: it is not my family's responsibility to fulfill me. They can't. They will never be able to. At the same time, I have also learned that it is not happiness or unhappiness I seek, but contentment.

And where I have found contentment is in my own spiritual practice (writing, reading inspiring books, listening to music, meditating, working out —whatever uplifts me) and in any work I put myself into that has meaning for how I want to give to the world.

What we need to remember, at some point, is that we all come from the same place. Just as I am a part of The U, so is everyone else. And if we remember that we all come from something loving and good (which I believe to be true), then something loving and good is always going to show up in our lives. That's how powerful we are. No matter how hard we try to feel miserable and create more drama in our lives, there is always a little reminder to remember where we really come from. No matter how crappy our life looks or how terrible our family seems to us or how awful we might feel about ourselves or others, there is a part of us that still creates small, external miracles that give us hope.

Of course, I struggle and go through tough times like everyone. But contentment always returns when I am able to remember where I really come from, when I am able to love myself a little bit more, when I'm able to return my control over to where it belongs by letting go and trusting life.

So, with all of that being said...as much as we want to be loved and accepted by our family members, they too want the same exact thing. And you will never know for sure how the other feels or where they are coming from until you can communicate with an open heart. So much heartache and suffering happens as a result of assuming things about family members and what we perceive to be a lack of acceptance of us — and yet so often what we assume is as far from the truth as anything. That is why tough conversations are so important. Take this example from the letters my mom and I wrote to each other about the day I came out, ten years after the fact:

Dear Mom,

I remember the day. The day I told you that I was gay. I had been with a woman for a year by then, and hiding it from you was so painful that I needed to get it out there...out of me. With uncertainty and a bit of courage, it seemed as though the road paved itself as your house inched closer, one block of concrete at a time. I drove from my house to yours, tears lodged in my throat...making their way to my eyes as my anxiety rose. I was so afraid. So afraid of what you would think. After disconnecting myself emotionally from you for a year, I was so distant from all that I knew, and I needed to find a way back home—back home to whoever I was missing behind my jumbled self-doubt. I was making a sincere leap and a desperate attempt to find myself by coming to you. Hoping you would have the answers.

When I arrived at your house on that hot, sunny Mississippi August day, you were outside in the garage. I think I remember you talking to someone who was leaving. As I got out of the car and walked towards you, you could tell that something was wrong. You asked me, "What's wrong? Are you okay?" My tears were fighting for their life, but I think that what had been buried for so long could not sit another moment inside of me, and so they began to stream down my face — my innocent face. I was so young and had just begun to open my eyes to the crueler side of people. You put your arms around me and led me to the living room. I could sense that you were unsure and confused about the reason for my tears. I was unsure too.

As we sat down on the couch, I finally uttered a few words: "I am not who you think I am. I am different than most girls." I remember when your confused expression turned into a fearful one once you realized what I was trying to say. I remember it like it happened yesterday. And maybe that's why

I need to write this now...to move on, to let go of that moment. I have been holding this tightness in my chest, as we have never talked about this time —never consciously moved through it together. For the past several years, we have grown into a duo of trust again, a duo of connection, our mother-daughter bond has grown to new heights...beyond understanding, because we were never able to really understand —we had to leap higher than that. I pushed you, and you pushed me, and we got here together. But I want to move further still, and that will require that this day—"the day"—be forgotten as the worst day of my life and embraced as the best. I am ready to let go, and somewhere inside of me I know you are too. We are the same, the two of us, the same behind our fears, the same behind the need to be loved, the same behind it all—behind it all, we are the same.

On that day, on the couch, when you began to cry—my world shattered. My heart broke as I realized I could never be who you wanted me to be. Or at least, that is how I took it. You said it before I could: "You mean, you are gay?" I nodded in dismay while behind your blank stare you processed the unwelcome information. You were my biggest mirror. I grew more and more silent, more and more distant as I realized that you weren't going to be able to give me what I needed.

Self acceptance has been a battle since that day for me. The deepest parts of me have been longing to let go of the rejection I have placed on myself over the years since then, from that one moment. And I feel that if I can heal this time in my life then something will shift for me. To that you would say, "Do it for you, Meagan, not for me. Let go and just love who you are." I am trying, really. You have told me that over the last few years, and with every new change I take another step, and each step has led me here—to openly acknowledging that you let me down that day. I translated your fear into rejection. You didn't embrace me the way I had hoped—you embraced me, but your confusion reflected my own. And there we were, two people who loved each other tremendously, suddenly foreign to one another—like we abruptly jumped into a past life that vaguely made some sense, but not enough sense. You hugged me when I left, after Dad and the boys had come over to share in the big surprise, but it wasn't the same. I left with a weight lifted but in its place I wondered if we would ever make it back to the day before "the day."

We gritted our teeth as we tried to move forward. I know I put up a wall, and I am sorry for that. I am sorrier that I couldn't give you the daughter, the woman you had hoped I would be. There is a sorrow that I have kept stored over the last ten years, stored for right now. I noticed it was still lingering the other day when I couldn't enjoy a perfect moment...that there was still something inside that needed to come out. And, when I closed my eyes this morning and asked The U for some help, an image of "the day" popped into my mind immediately. I have long avoided this moment, today, as I have been afraid of feeling what I felt so long ago – that if I tell you that you let me down then we would be disconnected again. It is even harder to tell you that you let me down when I know you were just afraid in that moment, as I am sure you were re-living your own childhood memories of being bullied and made fun of, re-living your family breaking up, and not knowing what would be in store for me as an openly gay woman in Mississippi. I understand your fears now, but then, I didn't.

I know, Mom, I know that you cannot give me joy and fulfillment —that is not what I am asking for. In fact, I am not asking for anything. I know you love and accept all of me now, and all of the joy and fulfillment my life is blossoming into, and I know I see you now, and all the joy and fulfillment you are blossoming into. I just can't hold onto "the day" anymore. I needed to revisit it, actually re-live it from a space of knowing that it doesn't matter anymore. That day can no longer be what I remember, it doesn't fit who I see in front of me each time we visit....myself. I need and want to let you love all of me now.

And tonight, I look forward to our weekly dinner, with Clare and me, you and dad. I look forward to it more now than ever as I sit here realizing that in the days before "the day" that's what we used to do — have dinner together every week. Here we are again.

I love you,

Meagan

Dear Meagan,

It's almost like a dream when I think back to "that day." So much has been lived since then.

"Mom!" your voice cracked as you said it over the phone. I knew something was not quite right when I heard my name. My heart fell some and I thought, "Please, not right now Megs." Remember, I was in Jackson, Tennessee, with my dear friend Ann who was battling lung cancer? Ann didn't know me that day, which made it even harder to be there with her. I had been making those six-hour trips one day a week for some time, now knowing I would not be having many more.

"I need to see you as soon as you get home!" You were so insistent. I tried to put you off, but couldn't. On the ride home I could not think of anything that could be that urgent. I even called you back to try to get you to tell me over the phone, but you would not have it. Needless to say, the drive home was long and my heart was already heavy from being with Ann.

You met me at the house. You were so nervous. I felt bad for you, but in my mind I was thinking it's not as bad as she thinks. It can't be.

You sat down beside me on the couch and before you could get it out, "you don't really know me," you started to sob. My heart broke for you. I took you in my arms and then you told me. I cannot remember the exact words in how you told me that you were gay. I kind of shut down. I went numb. My ears started to ring. I could only think.... I need your Dad here with us. He has always been my rock and I needed him here to hold me up so I could gain strength from him to hold you up. I realized in that moment our lives would never be the same. Change was evident. I know that I told you that I loved you because that was what I was feeling...but the questions that were storming through my mind were deafening. I was so confused...you had had dates, boyfriends.....my mind was reeling. I was shaking with disbelief.

When I looked at you and saw your pain, my heart broke for you. I then felt fear for you. What will everyone think? What will they say or do to you? Fear set in, and it stayed heavy in my heart for a very long time. I had to protect you!! No one was to know!

I remember calling your brothers and Dad and pleading with them to come home. I needed all of us to be together. I needed my family. YOU needed your family! I felt an urgency for us to be one and tell each other no matter what happens next that we love each other and will not turn our backs on each other. I needed to hear that as bad as you did. I went through that with my family with divorce, as you know, and I knew I could not bear it again.

That day was the beginning of a new life for all of us. As hard as it has been, it has also been very rewarding and rich with love and understanding. I know that I am a better person and Mom for it. I truly live in the moment and cherish each opportunity that I can spend with my family —a true blessing. God has enriched our lives beyond measure and I am grateful that my heart is no longer heavy with fear, but with an amazing peace.

It took me a while, but I finally realized all I want to do is live in the truth and to love....let it be the way it is. God can take care of the rest!!!! I love you my dearest daughter.

You inspire me to embrace courage and be me,

Mom

Agreeing to write those letters —and then writing them —took immense courage and an underlying trust in each other. But I realized that I needed to go through this process with my mom to experience further healing —and she was on board without hesitation. We each wrote our letters without reading the other's, and when we were done we shared our letters and then had a conversation about them. I had no idea my mom had been in so much fear at the time —I knew she had had a little fear, but I had thought that mostly she was just disappointed in me. And she had no idea that I had felt rejected because of her fear —her fear that had been for me, not her. Together, we were able to put all the pieces together. All this time I had been carrying the day I came out as a day of complete and utter rejection, when in reality all she had wanted to do was love and protect me through it but didn't know how. By our communicating with honesty and openness, I was able to leap over a huge wall that had been standing in my way all those years.

It's not about being gay —I don't think it matters what the issue is, every parent and child goes through similar things. Parents tend to fear for their child (the instinct is to protect), and children tend to feel rejected very easily by their parents. In my case, I found that my mom was mirroring to me my own insecurities, and now I feel like I can work with that.

She never rejected me at all...she was just afraid for me. But I would have carried that load of rejection until the day I died unless I had said something.

As my mom and I were closing our conversation about our letters, my mom said with such conviction, "I love you. I love you. I love you, Meagan. I don't know how else to let you know that I love you...as you are." This time, I let it in.

CHAPTER 6

Taking Action Will Set Us Free

Duty is a very personal thing. It is what comes from knowing the need to take action and not just a need to urge others to do something.

—*Mother Teresa*

A few years ago, when my book *Creating Your Heaven on Earth* was just published, I was on my way to upstate New York for a book signing and speaking engagement. This was my first book signing in a city where no one knew me — a writer's dream.

I was flying from Denver to Pittsburgh and then from Pittsburgh to Syracuse. I had an early flight to catch on the day of the book signing, which was scheduled for 6:30 that evening. I barely made the 30-minute cut-off to check in and had to run to my gate. I caught the flight, but just barely. The

flight went smoothly. I was so full of anticipation and excitement that feeling exhausted was fine by me.

My flight arrived in Pittsburgh on time. I made my way to
the "departure" board to check on the gate assignment for my
next flight. When I looked up at the board and found my flight,
bright red letters stared back at me: "CANCELLED." My heart
dropped. I started to panic on the inside. I was on the verge
of uttering a curse word or two out loud when a voice from my
heart said, "Meagan, go with the flow." I listened.

It turned out that numerous flights had been cancelled
to New York because of an ice storm. I decided that the result-
ing madness, frustration, and anger that hung in the air at
the airport was something I didn't want to be a part of. So I
listened instead to my inner voice and chose to go with the
flow and be who I wanted to be in the situation —which meant
being nice to everyone, seeing the best in everyone, being
calm and patient, and understanding that I might have to miss
the event in upstate New York that I had so wanted to attend. It
was a quick shift of mindset but a significant one.

I waited in line at the US Airways counter, at the gate for
my now cancelled flight. In front of me was a woman screaming in angry rage at the woman behind the desk. I felt so bad
for the US Airways agent —I mean, was she the one who had
caused the bad weather? After listening to the woman in front

of me do her best to make the agent feel awful, I made an extra effort to be nice to her when it came my turn.

"Thank you for waiting on me, and I promise I won't scream at you," I said to the agent. She smiled, and I could see her take a breath. I explained to her my dilemma. For several minutes, she did her best to find me another flight, but every available flight was leaving Pittsburgh after my event in New York was to have started. We looked at each other in disappointment, and I slowly felt myself letting go and giving in to the thought, "Well, I guess I just won't make it and there must be a good reason for it." Suddenly, the agent said, "I know!" She yelled across the terminal and asked another US Airways agent, "Did that flight leave yet?" He yelled back, "No!" She quickly printed out a ticket for me and told me I was going to Ithaca, about 60 miles from my event. I called my event coordinator, and arrangements were made for a driver to pick me up there.

I walked over to the new gate and stood there for about 30 minutes, wondering if I was in the right place —and wondering what in the world was going on, as there was no-one else at the gate but me. Eventually, another agent came up to me and asked, "Are you ready to go?" Confused, I said, "To Ithaca, right?" He nodded his head yes, and asked me to follow him outside. He took out his umbrella and walked me to the plane, about 20 yards away, and said, "You know you are the only one on this flight, right?" Wha-wha-whaaaaaaat?

Sure enough, I was the only person on the flight. The flight attendant greeted me and let me choose my seat, and as I sat down and buckled up, the pilot spoke over the loud-speaker, "Welcome Meagan, we are taking you to Ithaca. Sit back and enjoy the ride." Huh? Really? I guess there was a break in the clouds or something—kind of like the parting of the Red Sea.

I made it in plenty of time for my event that night. I will always be thankful to US Airways for the valuable lesson I learned that day —that choosing who you want to be in what may seem like an impossible circumstance, then taking action, and then letting go and going with the flow are the three ingredients that will open you up to life's miracles. Letting go is just as important as choosing who you want to be in situations that may seem tough, because the only real control we ever have is in that choice and the actions we take as a result.

Taking action based on who you want to be and then letting go sets us free. When Clare and I first moved to Columbus, Mississippi, we started off living in a house that was really cheap. It was directly across the street from our offices, and it was a good deal! There was a down side, of course, and that was that it was an older house with wall units, and the first winter after moving in we discovered the heating system was not so great. I noticed that I was getting sick regularly due to the dust and other allergens around, and I felt like we really needed to find another place to live. So we backed out of our lease and started looking. Our landlords rented the place much quicker than we had anticipated, and we were given a deadline of less than a month to move out. We could have chosen to resent this sudden deadline and see it as a hardship, but we knew by then that when life hands you things like deadlines you weren't expecting, there's a reason for it. In the end, it was a blessing, as it forced us to make a decision much faster.

We started by increasing our budget by half — surely we would come upon an awesome house for that much. But we couldn't find a thing. We looked and looked, and nothing was happening easily. We had agreed that we would not get a house that we both didn't absolutely want. Through the grapevine, we heard about a house on the river (I have always wanted to live on the river), but it was way outside our budget. I begged Clare for us to at least go look at it, so we did. We drove up and marveled at the landscape—the trees, the water, the wildlife—and knew immediately that we wanted to be there. We didn't need to look at the house, and we didn't care about the price.

We called the landlord immediately and told him we wanted the house. Tripling our budget was a scary leap for us —like, really scary. I mean, our businesses were doing well, but we had debts to pay off still. Could we really do this? Did we *deserve* something like this? The owner agreed to enter into a rent-to-own contract, and we sealed the deal.

We had a lot of discussions leading up to the decision to rent-to-own that house, but when it came time to either take it or leave it, we both knew we had to follow our gut, which was telling us to make the leap. The moment that finalized it for both of us was when I said, "If we want to take our business and our lives to the next level, we have to move there." We both knew the truth in that statement and from that moment we couldn't turn back. We knew that in order to move forward we needed to be in an environment that pushed us to see the beauty inside ourselves. I really wanted a writing space to do some important personal work, and we both wanted to experience more of a flow of abundance in our lives, so we knew that moving into a space that represented that for us was important, no matter how scary the leap. We adjusted our budget, took out our vacations for the year and saw that we could do it. We took the leap, and boy, did the healing begin —almost instantly.

From the moment we moved into the house, there was a part of me that knew and accepted that I deserved it. It was extremely hard at first to let all of that love in —but the love wanted to enter so badly, and so, little by little, I opened myself up to it. Every morning I wake up now, I feel like a queen. And the more I have gotten to know that part of me, the less I am able to tolerate anything that stands in its way. Now, when something shows up, I see it fairly quickly, I work through it, I cry about it, I learn from it, and I move on...back to the space of really enjoying what's around me. I simply cannot put into words how grateful I am for this house. It may seem like a material thing, but it's so much more than that: the beauty that surrounds me on the outside has been a reflection of my soul, and it has nurtured me and shown me how to find a way back to me — back to believing in myself and knowing I deserve all that my heart desires.

Since living in this house, I've learned so much about both vulnerability and letting go — and I've also learned that letting go is in and of itself an action. Over the last six months, I have written a lot and worked through a lot — mostly through my blog. My blog readers who follow me only see bits and pieces of my experience; what they don't see is that my blog has challenged me more than I had ever anticipated. As the days go on, I feel cleansed, I feel open, I feel motivated, and most of all, I feel really confident. It's as though through my willingness to be vulnerable and let go through the act of blogging, I have gotten over the hump of my past. I am always having dreams that lead me, guide me, and give me confidence in embracing something different for my life.

In the end, though, you know what got me to a place of letting go? A blog comment I received one morning. As I was reading it, the tears started to roll. It was from a person who is gay, and it is said:

> I get it...fully and completely...I feel the exact same way...and not just about marriage...it is so hard to put ourselves out there knowing that we are going to get shot down and rejected and sometimes by the people who we care about the most and knowing how to be confident enough and strong enough in our own skin to be able to say yes this is me like it or not and yes this is the person I want to live my life with and I want you all to know it is one of the scariest things out there...I live in Oklahoma and face a lot of the same issues you do there and I think that only compounds that struggle...but thank you for putting into words what I know so many of us are feeling!!

This comment struck me because it validated something for me. It helped me see that yes, the struggle has been hard for me. Really hard. And instead of battling the struggle, I can just let myself acknowledge that YES, it's tough. It's tough, damn it. I have done the very best I can. It has been enough. I am enough. I have done the very best I can, and it's okay. I am not alone here.

Sometimes it's important for us to acknowledge that we have struggled, and to acknowledge the courage it has taken for us to get where we are. We all have a struggle that pops up in layers, and we work through it. It's okay to struggle, and it's important to acknowledge it, to honor ourselves for our courage and then let it go and move on.

What has entered my life through all of my struggling is a belief in myself again. Moving into our new house has been a struggle — a good one, but a struggle nonetheless, as it has forced us to redefine who we are and that we deserve whatever we wish for. And through this struggle, something inside of me has opened — and I'm not sure it would have if we had stayed in our first house. It's been a long time, folks, and I can see that I am craving deeper connections with those around me. Yes, another door has opened in my heart.

Miracles happen when you take action on something you believe deep inside. Taking the leap in moving into this house has paid off on so many levels. Not because I live in a cool house and now I might look cool to others, but because the land around this house has gifted me with a love I have always felt deep within me. Not only that, but we have paid off more debt in the last six months than in the last five years! To be able to see life's abundance each day has really allowed me to work on embracing it further. I am so proud of our house—of our life. Most of all, I'm proud of me, and I know I will grow prouder still. In fact, one day recently I stated something in my blog I had never felt before: "I am proud to be gay." It's hard being gay, but I wouldn't change it at all. There's nothing I would change in my life. I'm proud of it, and I am even prouder to be me.

When your heart wants something, follow it. Take any action you can take, and let go of the rest. Your heart will lead you exactly where you want to go —and beyond. It might take a little work, a lot of digging deep, a few tough conversations, a lot of self-realizations, and a lot of trust in the unknown, but don't waiver! Follow your heart.

When you follow your heart, life will give you plenty of opportunities to continue to choose the path you truly want to follow. I was given such an opportunity when the Supreme Court (SCOTUS) made its rulings in June 2013 around Proposition 8 and the Defense of Marriage Act (DOMA).

I remember having a mix of both joy and fear after the SCOTUS rulings. I'm sure that for most gay Mississippians—I know for me—their coming-out experience was traumatic on some level. When decisions like the ones made by the

Supreme Court happen, old wounds are opened because the conversation is brought to the forefront. For any oppressed community or group of people —black, Jewish, Catholic, Hispanic, Moslem, gay, it doesn't matter —it's not easy to talk about the fears that lurk behind our joy. And while I was excited about the rulings, the feeling that "the other shoe is about to drop" still lingered. Mostly, though, I think we are afraid of our light. I knew I was being called in this moment of the SCOTUS rulings on gay marriage to rise higher than ever—just as we all are in moments like these.

In Mississippi, our history of oppression and segregation still hangs thick in the air. Let's be honest, no-one likes to talk about things that are painful. I get it. But in order to heal, we must have those painful discussions. To those of you who oppose gay marriage—we are in the same boat. Afraid. I'm afraid. You are afraid. I'm afraid of being rejected as gay marriage becomes more of a hot topic here, and you're afraid because it questions your beliefs about marriage—that it should remain as it is. But if you put fear and fear together, the result is tension, avoidance, anger, the feeling of injustice, and the need to be right by pointing outward rather than in. The same is true of any issue that separates us and causes us to discriminate against others.

We can't hold onto old wounds. We have to let go. Where there is fear, there is also love. They are the same but expressed differently, two sides of the same coin; it's our choice which one we want to look at.

As soon as SCOTUS made its decisions regarding DOMA and Prop 8, the local news station called me. They wanted to interview me on my thoughts, and they even asked Clare to come along. Some moments in life seem bigger than others, turning points where you know the decision you make then will affect your course in a significant way. Fear, although it was present, took a back seat in that moment, to the deeper and stronger knowing that in the entire universe we were exactly where we were meant to be right then. There was no hesitation at all—I was doing the interview. Clare didn't hesitate either. I had learned by now that to make any choice other than that of my heart was not an option for me. This is who I am: I will speak what is on my heart when I am asked to. Take it or leave it.

When Clare and I arrived at the station, we were greeted with hugs and acceptance. One of the news anchors came out to greet us specifically to hug me and compliment me on my blog. In Mississippi —a black straight woman hugging a white gay woman as a fellow human being. Mississippi's history may be just what you think it is —dark, complicated, and full of oppression—but we don't have to be our history anymore. Each one of us is only what we choose to be in each individual moment, and that can be exactly what our history has been — or it can be something different. My history (my coming-out experience) is what I think it was, but I am not my history anymore. I choose something different now. I believe in myself now, and I believe in the best of others.

Moving on from our past with its suffering and victimhood involves our deciding in each moment to experience and be something different — and then taking action on that decision. Mississippi is made of people who are loyal, hospitable, family oriented, and full of love and faith. My good experiences have far outweighed the bad, it's just that the bad experiences were so deeply hurtful that it has taken time for that hurt to transform. The person who interviewed Clare and me that morning said that she had called numerous couples to interview along with us and they had all declined. She said they were worried about their jobs, etc. I understand. We are not protected by the law here. I totally get it. In fact, it hurts to know that the gay community is still living in that fear. On the flip side, though, it was just as hard for them to find a preacher who was willing to be interviewed. We are all just afraid of being rejected, cast aside, not heard. Let me say this: if you are afraid of us "gays" being allowed to get married and what that might mean — we are equally afraid of you. Fear arises from fear, and fear begets fear. But as Gandhi said, "An eye for an eye makes the whole world blind."

We must be willing to have the difficult conversations. We have to talk — to talk not to change one another but to find a way to embrace all of the differences within our culture. Fear is habitual. True love NEVER feels the need to change others. That works both ways.

My vision for my life – and for everyone – is to have the opportunity to be who I am fully, with no fear attached. Maybe I am dreaming, but I believe somebody has to. And the only way to bridge the gap of fear is to rise above it to where love resides, and to act from that place. It's the only way.

The interview about the SCOTUS rulings on Prop 8 and DOMA gave me an opportunity to see how far we have come both as a society and within our own culture here in Mississippi. I was extremely nervous for the interview to air, as you never know what clips they are going to show from the entirety of the actual time you spent talking on camera. Overall, they did a great job. And while I was afraid of the response on one level, another part of me knew that we were less likely to get a negative response than a positive one. Taking action on where my heart led me that day helped heal not only me but others as well. Here are some of the things we heard after the interview:

—From a preacher friend in the grocery store: "So, what kind of response are y'all getting from your interview?" I said, "It has been all positive so far." With a big grin on his face, "Well, praise the Lord."

—From one of Clare's patients: "I saw you on TV the other night. I am so happy for you."

—From a friend: "I feel like I can do anything after seeing y'all do that interview!"

—From someone we have never met: "I know I don't know you, but kudos for going on WCBI last night. I know how risky it was, although you were already out. I hope you and your partner experience only good things from it."

—From a blog reader: "Great job on the WCBI interview. You represent Columbus well."

—From another reader: "Whatever I can do to help. Equality now."

—From another reader: "Very thoughtful. You really gave me some things to think about. You are an exceptional communicator."

—From about 20 others of Clare's patients and my clients: "I am so proud of y'all. Congratulations!"

—From a random woman on Main Street in Starkville on a busy Friday night: "Hey I saw y'all on TV the other night. I am so happy for y'all! Congratulations!" She reached out to shake both of our hands and continued to tell the group of people she was with about us.

　　—From another random woman that we had never met: She shakes both of our hands and says, "How about the Supreme Court! Woo hoo!"

Taking action sets you free. When you are willing to take the risk and put yourself out there, to speak from love and your own experience, there will always be a positive response. Sometimes that response will be subtle, sometimes loud, but The U always responds in kind to whatever it is that you put out. This is especially true during those times when you feel called to do something but are afraid to do it. Clare and I didn't have one negative thing said to us after doing the above interview. We did it because we felt called to, but especially because we had been told others were afraid to. And if we can do it, you can too. Even more beautiful is that when you are willing to allow yourself to be vulnerable—and expose your vulnerability—others are given permission to be vulnerable too, and deeper, more meaningful connections and relationships will result.

CHAPTER 7

Rising Above Right and Wrong

As long as you keep a person down, some part of you has to be down there to hold him down, so it means you cannot soar as you otherwise might.

—Marian Anderson

I remember walking my dog a couple of years ago in the neighborhood Clare and I used to live in. We had on sweats, normal walking attire for cold weather. We weren't holding hands or walking abnormally close together—we were getting in a workout. A truck drove by pretty fast, with two college-age-looking guys in it. They rolled down their windows as they drove by and yelled out, "lesbians!" and laughed. It took me a minute to gather what had just happened.

If someone else had told me this story, I would have said, "I can't believe those idiots. Who do they think they are?" But when it's you, the game changes. I may have tried to prepare myself for things like this, but when things happen suddenly and you don't expect them, it gives you a good feel for where you are in your life. After processing the incident for a few minutes, a fire started to go off inside my chest as I went through all the things I would have liked to have yelled back. But then I realized, wait, I *am* a lesbian. Hold on, how should I feel about this? I mean, should I be thankful that they didn't throw rocks or a beer can at us? Was their statement one of hate? Or were they just being young and silly? They didn't say, "I hate lesbians!" For all I know, they have a bunch of gay friends and are totally cool with it. Or what if I wasn't a lesbian and they were just making an assumption? And on and on and on...

Our thoughts can lead us down crazy-making paths. This incident reminded me that I can only know and control my own reaction. I can't control other people. The truth is that we never really know all the sides to any story, no matter how clear it may seem to us in the moment. In this instance, I got angry initially, but then a minute or two rolled by and I was able to let it go. I realized quickly that what my anger really was, was a shield that was trying to protect a feeling of rejection that lay underneath — and once I was aware of that I was able to let my guard down. Ultimately, it didn't matter how or why those boys said what they said, or even what they meant —what I needed to listen to was how I reacted and what my reaction was telling me about me. What I learned from this experience was, *I don't want to be* that person who drives that truck and yells at people and leaves behind confusing messages, but I also learned that sometimes the confusion is in me.

Ultimately, it doesn't matter who is right and who is wrong, what matters is my own experience and what I decide to do to make it better or worse for me. I want to be responsible for the energy I put out and give to other people. In this instance, the best way I know how to do that would be to put on my sweats and go on another walk with my partner, waving to every truck that drives by with two college boys in it (well, and other cars too).

We spend so much time and energy worrying about others' impressions of us, as if the way others feel about us is the "right" way and we have to figure out how to fit into it. I have clients all the time who make excuses for not speaking their truth, not saying what they really want to say for fear of being rejected. My response is always this: you will never know how someone will respond unless you give them the opportunity. Most situations are both right and wrong, it just depends on how you choose to look at it. If you go around trying to get the "right" response from everyone, you'll never discover or honor who you truly are — or who they are. Sometimes people will hurt you, and sometimes they will pleasantly surprise you, but you have to be willing to take the risk of either if you want to be yourself. And ultimately, your fear of others' opinions just keeps them locked up and condemned in your mind. I have been hurt before—I have had people reject me and attack me verbally — but I have chosen to move through that hurt and give people a chance again. I am not always open immediately, but when I am afraid to speak up or add to the conversation, then that is a cue for me to look at myself and figure out what I need to do to build my confidence in who I am and who I want to be.

Differing opinions are what help us grow, to open our eyes to other perspectives and be challenged in a way that helps us figure out more of who we are as an individual. Different is just that, different — it doesn't have to mean wrong. If you feel attacked by rude comments about liberals, Democrats and President Obama, then it might be wise to surround yourself with people who think like you do until you are able to put yourself in that kind of group again without feeling "less than." Our experience and reaction to things is *always* our responsibility. There is no-one else to take the blame. Comments may be rude, but our reaction to them doesn't have to be —and if we feel attacked, it is because we are allowing ourselves to feel "less than."

Being a minority or feeling oppressed by a larger group of people is a mindset, and overcoming that mindset is not for the weak at heart; it is for those with the utmost courage. Overcoming the mindset of victimhood is an opportunity to test your courage and strength, to see if you can face your fear and see what results. You might be accepted or rejected for what you say, but the only thing you are responsible for is how you say what you want to say and if you feel good about it. Beyond that, everything else is out of your control. You are the master of your own perception of yourself, and keeping people from getting to know the real you deprives both them and you and closes you off from receiving love from others.

Our truth is what's right for us in any given moment. It's who we are deep down inside. Once you figure that out, life is no longer about right or wrong, it's just about being authentic. Figure out who you want to be, and then be it; that is your truth. That is what is "right" for you. The fear of speaking our truth is always that we will be rejected and, as a result, feel unloved and not good enough. Sometimes just acknowledging our fear will push us forward; if you know what is keeping you from speaking your truth, then it might be easier to overcome. The more confidence you have in who you are, the easier it will be to let go of others' reactions to who you are, and the easier it will be for you to accept others' truths.

Speaking your truth takes courage. You may not be able to speak up immediately, and that's okay. It's important not to judge yourself while you are learning to be okay with who you are —judging just puts you back in the place of right or wrong. Sometimes it's good to just observe how you are feeling and realize that no-one is personally attacking you with their own opinions about politics or religion. Opinions are only opinions, and most of us protect them vehemently but only because we don't want to make ourselves wrong —the intention isn't to attack, it's to protect ourselves. If someone is being overly judgmental and you can't handle it any longer, just don't continue to put yourself in that position. They are defending themselves because they don't want to be wrong, that's all. You always have a choice, always.

If you want to overcome your fear and find a way to share your opinions with confidence, without making the other person wrong, then the way to start is by doing things for yourself that make you feel good about you —exercising, writing, singing, meditating, helping someone, etc. It doesn't matter what gives you confidence, just commit to doing it once a day, and it will make a huge difference. By building up your own confidence, you will be able to speak from a new place, a place where no-one has to be wrong but all can appreciate the others' thoughts. Remember, you never know how someone will respond unless you give them the opportunity.

We have all been told our whole lives what to believe, what is right and what is wrong – by our families, our churches, our cultures, our friends, our teachers, the media, the books we read, and so on. But we are rarely taught to just listen to what our heart is telling us – the place beyond right and wrong, the place where truth resides.

Unfortunately, because I am gay and grew up in Mississippi, the group of people that has discriminated against me the most is Christians. In the name of God, I have been called a criminal for being gay, been suddenly shunned and ignored, received hate calls, and been told that I am going to hell and I deserve it. It used to be that if I ran into some-one I knew was a "devout" Christian, I would turn and walk in another direction. But if I couldn't ignore the person then I would find a way to shy away from questions like, "So, are you married?" or "So, do you have a boyfriend?" It was easy enough to hide this part of my life because I don't wear being gay on my forehead. We all know that feeling, no matter what it is we may be hiding in order to escape possible rejection — it is the feeling of shame, the feeling of being less than.

Eventually, I grew out of escaping those questions. I hoped for a long time that I would be strong enough one day to love and accept those who rejected me along the way. At least, I believed it was possible —and today I not only know it is possible, I try to live it daily. Some days, I'm not totally there, but my perspective continues to shift. I try to realize in each moment what kind of person I want to be, and I know and acknowledge that it requires taking time to love, appreciate, and discover who I am.

We cannot forever blame whoever we feel is our oppressor —we cannot forever be victims. When we make someone else wrong and ourselves right, we get stuck in a cycle of victimhood and oppression. Trust me, it's easy for me to slip into a victim mentality, blaming the whole world and every Christian I come across for my lack of equality because of bad experiences with other Christians. But I would rather choose to put my energy on other things, things that don't make others wrong or me right. After all, to blame all Christians for the mistakes of a few is not only unfair, it's ridiculous —and yet we all do just that. We generalize entire groups of people and set ourselves up to be victims over and over again. I hope that one day I will be able to marry my partner and be treated equally and fairly by all —but I also know it starts with me. And it starts with me by being who I really am —because when we build relationships based on love —which is what we all truly are —then we are able to open both our own and each other's eyes and hearts.

Moving back to Mississippi took more courage than anything else I have done, because it was a choice to rise above right and wrong —which meant I had to let go of my victim-hood and "rightness." It was a choice to move here so that I could try to love those who hated me before. What I have real-ized in the process is that as a result of loving myself more, I am now surrounded only by people who love, support, and encourage me. Has it been an internal battle? Oh, yes. Have I experienced discrimination? Yes, most definitely. But I wouldn't exchange it for all the gold in the world. And by choosing to love the Christians who despise me, what I see more of are the Christians who are willing to understand me, willing to love me, willing to try.

Let's not lose sight of thanking those who support us and accept us—those who stand up for us. Sometimes they come in the strangest disguises. In fact, I want to thank those who have rejected me too: Thank you for pushing me to be stronger, to claim more of what I want to surround myself with, and for showing me the path to the door where my healing and recol-lection of who I really am reside. I believe I needed each one of you. If you call me a criminal for being gay and I retaliate by calling you ignorant, then I am no better than you. I am no better than you anyway, just different. It isn't my responsibility to decide who you are meant to be, only to honor your path as your own and mine as mine. If you want to hate me, I can choose to walk away and be around someone who tells me I am wonderful just as I am. I don't have to be with you if you don't want to be with me. Your right may be my wrong, but neither is ultimate truth. All I can do in any moment is what is most right for me, and that is to be who I am underneath it all.

The truth of the matter is, if we seek love we will find it...and if we seek what we call hate or ignorance, then we will experience more of it. If you believe you aren't consciously seeking hate or ignorance, then take a look around you and see what you are reading or watching, and who you are spending your time with. If your company and your choices inspire you to love, then you are seeking love; if they inspire you to hatred and conflict, then you are seeking those. All I am saying is let's rejoice in the ones who support us, let us thank and embrace our supporters, let us acknowledge those who make it hard for us, and let us move forward. The more attention we put on those we think are keeping us from what we want, the more it will keep us from getting what we really want—freedom.

Over the years, my mom and I have worked hard on our relationship. It was tough on her when I told her I was gay. It took me time to see that, but that's what I see now — not that she was unsupportive but that she was having a hard time. She is as human as I am. Honesty and communication have been key to the success of our relationship.

A few years ago, right after returning from a vacation, I sat in the kitchen with mom and suddenly began to cry. I cried because I was letting go...letting go of the past. I felt as though I had been trying too hard to gain everyone's acceptance by taking on too much, instead of just being myself. My mom stood in front of me without my having said a word, looked me in my eyes, put her hands on mine, and with complete unconditional love said, "Let it go. Be who you are." She didn't understand my tears, because I had not told her what they meant; she went to a place outside of herself, and only love came through.

That interaction has healed many layers for me. I realize we aren't all fortunate enough to have a mom like I do. But there is someone who will tell you those exact words: "Let it go. Be who you are." It might be a voice inside your heart or a knowing that can't be misplaced by any negativity. There are resources everywhere for you. If I could say that to every person around the world who is hurting and feeling like they will never be able to move past the discrimination they continue to experience, I would take the time to do so. In fact, let me do so now: "Let it go. Be who you are."

Throughout my journey, in my darkest moments and my toughest hours, somewhere outside of me there was always a light shining in the heart of another showing me the way, re-introducing me to the goodness of the human spirit. If it is tough for you now, I know there is someone who can be that light for you until you can be that light for yourself. Trust the Universe, be yourself, love yourself and others as best you can, and ultimately that is what you will attract back to you.

The common thread of all religions is love...to love ourselves, our God (whoever that is or however It may look to you), and others. The contrasts and differences we experience in our world serve a purpose; they show us what is important to us and invite us to expand our experience. It is up to each one of us as individuals to determine and then be who we want to be.

I make a great effort to continually remember the love I have received from so many Christians and so many others from all walks of life and religions over the years. Thank you for embracing me so I could learn to embrace myself and move on from a feeling of being less than to a feeling of empowerment. Now I know I can embrace others, and I can embrace in my heart those who continue to reject me. What used to be

"I'm gay, unless you're Christian," is now "I'm Meagan, and it's so nice to meet you."

I was given a wonderful opportunity to "walk my talk" shortly after moving back to Mississippi. A local television station called me one morning and asked if I would be willing to come in and talk about my perspective on same-sex commitment ceremonies being allowed in state buildings. This conversation was a hot topic at the time because a same-sex couple had recently applied to have a commitment ceremony in a state building in Jackson, Mississippi. This hadn't gone over well with most people, but there was no law in place to keep the couple's application from being dismissed. Ultimately, they were given permission to have their ceremony, but most of the state was in an uproar. The television station wanted me to come on and talk about how this made me feel as an openly gay woman. They mentioned that they would be having someone else come on and talk with me, but they didn't tell me who.

I was completely terrified to say yes, so I said yes. I had learned by now that if I wanted to overcome my fears, I had to be willing to act when I felt them, so I said yes to the interview because I knew deep inside that I had to. My heart was pounding when I got off the phone. I was more nervous than I had ever been — in fact, I felt like throwing up — but the bigger part of me knew I could do it and that I could do it well. Besides, I had been consciously working on my own self confidence and had also realized that I felt called to speak out as an openly gay person in Mississippi in a loving way that represented my authentic self. So, after years of getting in touch with that part of me, I knew this was an opportunity for me to express myself in a way that was truly from my heart.

I knew that doing this interview was a turning point for me, and I was willing to risk the fear of the unknown in order to find more of myself. My fears were so deep that I was afraid I would walk out of that television station and someone would shoot me. That may seem unreasonable to some of you, but when you have been threatened and have seen others like you lose their lives because of their sexuality, those fears are very real.

Despite the fears, however, there was a part of me that was focusing on the bigger picture. As much as there is a part of me that wants to fight those I think can't see past my sexuality, and as much as I want to push those away who want to openly reject me, there is still a part of me that knows I would never be satisfied with that. That part of me is in everyone, the part of our human essence that sees everyone for who they truly are...different, unique, and equal. So I knew I was ready deep down, even though my fear of rejection on television was both real and validated by my past.

When I walked into the TV station, I looked to my left, and there sat a pastor from a Southern Baptist church. My heart sank from my chest down to my stomach, not because he was a Southern Baptist pastor, but because I knew him. We were friends — but he didn't know I was gay. Years before that, he had been the principal of a middle school where I had been working pro bono as a life coach with a lot of his students. We had had to work together to help these kids, and we had both seen the true part of the other through this work.

My fear grew deeper and deeper because now that I knew we would be interviewed together, the rejection could be greater for me — this wouldn't be just any other pastor rejecting me (there had been many before him); this time, it would be on air and with someone I knew. Talk about scared. I was literally shaking.

As we sat down on the set, we shared very little conversation. We were both nervous because neither of us had known that we would be speaking on this topic with the other. We were both extremely uncomfortable because it was clear that we cared for one another as people. There we sat, waiting for the cameras to roll: he, a pastor of a Southern Baptist church; the host, a congregate at his church; and I, the gay girl. The host told me not to be nervous, and I said, "It isn't the cameras that make me nervous." I had been interviewed many times before, but not like this. The producer assured me that this was to be an equal conversation and that she didn't want anyone to feel like they were backed in a corner. In my mind, it was two against one already, so I had to close my eyes and access the part of me that was saying, "Just be yourself and speak your truth. You are them, and they are you." After I opened my eyes the interview began, and in no time it was over.

Fear can cause you to either run away or dive so deep into yourself that you are able to access your authenticity... and that's what happened to me in that moment. I dove into the deep, uncomfortable, scary place that we often avoid, and I found myself.

Part of accepting your own equality in the world, the place beyond right and wrong, is accepting yourself. In the moment before the interview, that is exactly what happened: a space opened for truth to enter. I saw clearly that I was beautiful as I was, and that I could speak from my heart and not feel like I needed to protect myself, hide myself, or feel like I was victim to the situation. But to get there it took closing my eyes, accessing my heart, and choosing to only take responsibility for my own words and actions. That is true empowerment. Everyone has moments in their life when an opportunity for a turning point is given, and you can always choose to pass those opportunities up. I am so grateful that I didn't shy away from this opportunity. It changed the course of my life and it helped me see that my beauty may be different, but it is not less than anyone else's.

After the interview, I cried tears of relief. Relief that I had made it through, relief that I hadn't felt rejected, relief that I had realized I could choose to be a victim or not in any moment.

As long as I feel I am a victim in any situation, I will most likely choose to fight back, and that accomplishes nothing for me and leads any conversation to a halting point.

Watching the interview back, I see where I could have felt rejected (when the host alluded to my being a "good person" – almost like it was okay I was gay because I was a good person), but I didn't feel rejected in the moment. The lesson I learned from this interview was that if I want to accept myself, I need to make choices that are in alignment with who I really am and with who I want to be. Before watching it back, all I remembered saying from that short segment was: "I am only responsible for me. If I feel good about who I am at the end of every day, then that is all that matters to me."

And that's the truth. I cannot change another, and because I cannot change another then all of my energy can go into my own self-growth. Although I still sometimes want to put my fists up and explain myself or get people to see that being gay cannot be understood intellectually, I always remember this interview and how it taught me to put my fists down, to listen, and to speak my truth. At least now I know what is possible, and I have this example to fall back on when I feel like fighting back and making someone else wrong.

I have certainly had my own battles with what it means to be accepted as an equal by others. Getting to a point of realizing that I am not "less than" just because I am gay took time —and it is still a daily commitment —but the defining moment for me came when I realized that I am just different, that's just who I am, and choosing to be okay with it. That realization took personal work, and a lot of it.

We cannot be another. My partner and I cannot be a straight couple. A white man cannot be a black man. A child cannot be an adult. We have spent centuries trying to make others fit into our own boxes by destroying each other's uniqueness. Not all people try to change others with bad intent, but trying to change another can never end up feeling good for either party. We sabotage ourselves as a society when we think that our way is the only way. Our true nature is to love no matter what, and when we don't do that, we all suffer. There are ramifications to our actions of disagreeing with others. Whether I am a Christian disagreeing with the "lifestyle" of a gay person or a gay person disagreeing with the religious interpretation of a Christian, it ends up serving no-one. It serves no-one to reject the free will of another.

I don't believe in agreeing to disagree. I believe in moving past that, past right and wrong, to the place beyond opinions. I believe in conversation, conversations that lead to understanding and acceptance. I believe that every person should feel like a ROCK STAR because of who they are, inside and out —so much so that vulnerability doesn't have to be such a courageous act for so many.

Rising above right and wrong happens when you love who you are, when you act in alignment with who you are and know that your way is not necessarily the best way for everyone. We all have a place inside ourselves that whispers truth to us. That whisper of truth is what is right, and it whispers differently in each person's heart. When we live from our heart, right and wrong are irrelevant; all that matters then is that we follow our own truth and honor the right of others to do or not do the same.

Full-Circle Moments

After I completed this book, I was given the opportunity to experience three full-circle moments in succession. The first happened when I was invited to speak at Mississippi State University for National Coming Out Day. A series of spectacular, heart-breaking, heart-lifting, and door-closing events followed.

Live Out Loud, a nonprofit organization from New York, has a program called The Homecoming Project whose purpose is to help LGBTQ people go back to their old schools to share their story with other students. My publisher asked me at some point if I would be interested in connecting with Live Out Loud's Homecoming Project. After looking at the website, I didn't hesitate — I wanted to go back to one of my old schools to tell my story. I felt compelled to reach out to The Homecoming Project because I knew deep down that I wanted to be a voice for LGBTQ people in Mississippi—and not just a voice, but a positive one. The fact that Live Out Loud would help me set up my own homecoming project, and knowing that it would offer the support it did, made me want to work with them even more. Live Out Loud would also do the work of reaching out to the schools I had attended, which made the process much more attractive to me and gave me the courage to pursue it.

While the climate for LGBTQ people in Mississippi is slowly changing, we certainly still have a long way to go. It's not that people aren't accepting here—it's just that they haven't been called to task. The issues have been swept under the rug with all of our other Southern dirty laundry, and that is where they will remain until we have conversations…conversations that allow us all to get to know one another. The Homecoming Project allowed me to begin a conversation. It would have been so nice when I first came out of the closet to have had someone to talk to who understood me and could be a positive example for me. I never had that —which was exactly my motivation to want to be that. I knew I needed help reaching out, and this opportunity could do that for me.

I was connected quickly with an intern from The Homecoming Project who ended up working for an entire year trying to get a school in Mississippi to respond. While there are many LGBTQ people who live in Mississippi, we still do not have any rights under the law. Following a long period of no response, Mississippi State University finally said, "Yes." As a graduate from Mississippi State, this was both exhilarating news and the scariest news I could have ever received.

When I came out of the closet, as I've mentioned previously, I was a graduate student and an athlete at Mississippi State, and my experience had been one that was very hurtful. Shunned, ignored, put to the side, I had received hate voicemails, screaming phone calls, and meetings at the campus chapel with people I had called friends letting me know that I was going to hell and that I needed to get myself back on track. So to be given the opportunity to heal that time in my life ten years later was both liberating and completely nerve-racking.

Deep down, I wasn't surprised Mississippi State had said yes. I had known someone would say yes when the time was right. As frustrating as it may have been for the Live Out Loud staff to wait so long, I had known deep down that their efforts would pay off and that I would be ready when the call came. And I was ready.

From the time I had contacted Live Out Loud until the time of the actual event, a year had passed. During that year while I was "waiting," a lot had happened. I was able to be on TV twice to represent the gay community —once with a

Southern Baptist minister and another time with my partner, Clare. I was given opportunity after opportunity to build my confidence and clarify my message. During this time, I also reconnected with my blog and found my voice on a deeper level. Looking back, I can see why my own homecoming project needed time to brew...as I was brewing internally each and every day.

Leading up to my Homecoming Project experience at Mississippi State University, I knew I must prepare myself and go deep within, and so much of my time waiting was spent being quiet, taking opportunities when they landed in my lap, and healing layers upon layers of doubt and fear. Moving through my own emotions and feelings of the cultural climate, my own relationships, and where I was personally was no easy task. Patience is hard —and it demanded that I face many of my own fears of rejection.

I titled my talk for my Homecoming Project, "Courage: Agreeing to Disagree Is Not Enough." I chose this topic because the most popular thing I would hear when I first came out of the closet from people was, "I love you, Meagan, but I don't agree with being gay." From the moment I came out until the moment I stepped on the stage for my Homecoming Project, I had been working on loving myself and finding a way to love those who opposed me and still do, so that I wouldn't be someone who would say, "I love you, Bob, but I don't agree with the way you think being gay is wrong." I didn't want to be what others had been to me.

A few weeks before the event, I was extremely nervous and unsure of the response I might receive. But I had a faith in my community because of the support I had received over the course of the previous year. I am so grateful that many of these events in my life over that year were spread out proportionately so that I could grow and process accordingly.

The talk at Mississippi State was well attended and one of the proudest moments of my life. I was completely myself on stage for an hour. I didn't hold back. I began by reading an excerpt from this book:

> "Agreeing to disagree is not enough. It sends a message that one is better than the other — or at least, that's how I feel when I hear it. I believe we have to do better for our fellow people than agree to disagree, by encouraging them to be who they are, to be who they want to be, to be who they feel called to be, and to follow their heart on their journey. If we do that, then equality will happen naturally."

I then dove into my story and the many lessons I have learned on my journey. I talked about many of the stories I have covered in this book. I talked about how my mom and I wrote letters to each other about the day I came out of the closet—I wrote about my experience, and she wrote about hers —so we could both heal and move on. I talked about how from that experience I learned how important it is to have the tough conversations. I talked about being on TV with a Southern Baptist minister; about the miracle of catching my own private plane to upstate New York; about running into and learning to accept those who had hurt me before; about moving back to Mississippi when everything in me wanted to run the other way. And I talked about all of the lessons I have learned along the way, that taking action will set me free; that life is for me, not against me; that it's up to me to transform my pain into love; and that I am not a failure—I just am.

My talk at Mississippi State that night was a full-circle moment for me. And, as life would often have it, I was blessed to experience two more full-circle moments as a direct result of the first.

The second full-circle moment involved three people who were in the audience that night, Jayne and Dwight and their son, Nathan. Jayne and Dwight had been wonderful friends of my parents over the previous year, as they all shared something in common — both couples had a gay child and both were from Mississippi. It struck me, as I looked over the audience that evening, how amazing it was to have another proud set of parents there to support the event. It was especially good to see Dwight there, as I had never met him before.

A week later, my parents called and asked if Clare and I wanted to go to dinner with Jayne, Dwight, Nathan and his boyfriend. Our schedule was open, so we planned to meet them after work. On the way to dinner, I told Clare how amazing it felt to have the opportunity to go to dinner with my parents and another set of supportive parents of a gay child AND their child and his boyfriend. In Mississippi. A new experience for me.

Both sets of parents were just as excited to be casually going to dinner — to sit and be at peace with one another. There was no tension, no worry about who was around or what they may be thinking — just breaking bread and soaking in the laughs, the joy, the love, the acceptance, the understanding — the moment.

At one point during the meal, I caught Dwight staring at his son while he was talking to his boyfriend. He had a smile on his face — a smile filled with love and pride and support and acceptance and compassion. My eyes welled up with tears, as you can't mistake moments like these. They touch a part of you that is so deep, so real, and so true. The moment passed as quickly as it had come, but it remained with me. It was enhanced as I suddenly realized the same gaze in my parent's eyes—towards me. I thought, here are the eight of us, at a restaurant in a small town in Mississippi, breaking the perception that most people have…all proud of who we are and who we are with. Amazing. I left the evening with deep gratitude and an awareness of how special it had all made me feel.

The weekend passed, and on Monday morning I got a panicked call from my mom saying that Jayne had just found Dwight dead on their couch in their home. They believed that he had had a heart attack. In shock myself, I hustled over to their house to be of assistance with whatever needed to be done. I drove up and saw Jayne, my mom, and her sons. My heart dropped. There are moments in life when you know that no words will matter…when there is nothing you can do to make it better—and yet, the desire is so strong to want to fix it.

Life is a snapshot…but moments of love are eternal.

What I will remember about Dwight is the way he filled the room with love in my heart as he gazed at his son at dinner on his last Friday night—I'll remember it forever as if it had been me he was looking at.

Looking back, I am reminded of the fragile life we have been given—it comes and goes with the change of the seasons—so swiftly. Moments where we catch ourselves to soak it all in, to release all we think we know so we can embrace what is, are fleeting. Life is so short. We don't have time to wonder if others are okay with who we are. We don't have time to see if we are okay with how those we love are choosing to live their lives. We don't have time to think about who is right and who is wrong, who is better and who is worse. What we have time for is to let life in...to let it be exactly what it has been trying to show us for eons...itself.

May the sorrows of the world, the hurt, the self-induced pain, and the fear turn inward and become the truth—the truth of knowing we are so deeply loved and then to love others in that same capacity.

Death often forces us to let the light in by remembering what's important, only for that light to dissipate and often turn into fear. For me, this time, I hope my light will continue to grow so I too can one day gaze at those around me without them ever knowing just how much they are loved—just as Dwight did with his son.

My third full-circle moment was also made possible that night as I spoke on campus. In telling my story, I recounted how the Fellowship of Christian Athletes had been the one organization to discriminate against me the most. I didn't focus on blaming or pointing the finger, I just simply stated what had happened, how it had felt, and how I had grown as a person because of it.

After my talk, the local news put my story on the front page of the paper, and then the same article ran in Mississippi State University's campus paper. The response was outstanding. My mom ended up getting a lot of phone calls—as she is now one of my biggest supporters—from people wanting to reach out and say, "Hey, my sister is gay," "Did you know that my brother/son is gay?" People wanted to have a conversation—wanted to connect on a long-ignored subject in our small Southern town.

Through vulnerability there is connection. Because I was vulnerable in my talk, others felt compelled to be the same. Life's miracles are always waiting to be uncovered. But it didn't end there.

About three weeks after the event, I got a call from the current director of the Fellowship of Christian Athletes at MSU—a different director than when I was attending Mississippi State. He called me to officially apologize for what I had gone through ten years prior. He then invited me to his office to sit down and talk. I let it in—all I felt was gratitude and humility. I felt gratitude because I realized I was in a place to let the apology in and humility because I had waited for that moment for so long. It was that pivotal moment in your life when you feel like, "This is why I was born."

I had never expected an apology. I had never dreamt of an apology. But I had always hoped that a bridge could be built between the gay community and the more conservative Christian community in Mississippi. In this instance, because we were both willing to be vulnerable, a conversation was born.

When I got to his office, he met me at the door. He stuck out his hand to shake mine, and I opened my arms to imply a hug — and he met me there. Our chat began with the basics—where are you from, how did you get to where you are, and so on. His energy was calm and mine, calm too. He told me about his life, his faith, his faults…his story, and I told him mine.

His intention for the talk was to be able to apologize to me face to face…and that is what he did. He went on to ask me, "Meagan, how can I love you more?" — meaning, how can I, a conservative Christian love you, a gay woman, more?

I said, "What broke my heart when I came out of the closet is that people stopped seeing me for who I really was." I told him that growing up I had been very focused on what I had wanted out of life—I had always known who I was. I played sports, made good grades, had a small group of really good friends, and spent most of my free time writing about spirituality and God. When I went on to college I was the same: I never caused any trouble, never had a desire to fill a void with drugs or alcohol, and I focused on my studies, my sports, my spirituality and what I wanted out of life. As a part of the Fellowship of Christian Athletes, I got a spiritual outlet in the only way I knew to get it—there weren't a lot of options that I knew of at the time, so it was my spiritual community. But when I came out of the closet, I told him, that safe haven turned against me. It was as though who I was had been forgotten or misplaced, or even as if I had never existed. So I, a strong woman with a strong foundation, a normal childhood with no abuse of any sort, no desire to fill a void that I believe only some form of spirituality can fill...suffered. I can't imagine what people go through who have no support from their family, no spiritually sound foundation deep down, who have experienced abuse or neglect at some point in their life, or who don't have some sort of hope that life is on their side. I always knew life was on my side deep down, and I was determined to hold onto that belief even though I was being crushed at the time.

So my answer to him was simple: "I stopped being seen. I just wanted to be seen. We all deserve to be seen for who we really are."

He paused and said, "That's powerful."

He went on to tell me a few stories, and I told a few. I went on to talk about my own challenges, and he shared his. I jumped into saying how I feel like we have to move beyond agreeing to disagree and find a place between us where we can let go of our attachments to right and wrong—how if we can meet in that space there won't be a reason for apologies in the future...that there won't be a reason for tears and suffering around the subject. Perhaps we can coexist and support one another in that?

It was a simple conversation. A beginning of many, I hope.

I know that I was able to be present and confident, able to see him and his heart even though I know he still thinks (because he said so) that we disagree on theology. I don't disagree with his theology—I am just trying to move myself to a place where theology no longer matters, where we can simply see beyond the constructs we have made others out to be in order to see who they really are.

What I saw in him was a compassionate, curious, loving man. And what he saw in me, I hope, was forgiveness and an open heart.

I am a divine expression. He is a divine expression. There is nothing wrong with him. There is nothing wrong with me. I am loved. He is loved. We are the same. The rest just doesn't matter.

Because of The Homecoming Project, I was able to tell my story at Mississippi State University. I am now freer than ever before. I feel I have been catapulted into a new life even though I am still shedding the old one —the old stories, the old voices, the old lies. I have found me again —the belief in myself that I have so long searched for since I came out of the closet ten years ago. It is completely overwhelming. I am not sure what lies ahead for me now, but I can tell you one thing —it is going to be amazing.

After my talk at Mississippi State, Dwight's death, the director of Fellowship of Christian Athletes apologizing, and then my chat with him that followed, I decided I was ready to get married.

I never thought the day would come when I would be ready to get married. It wasn't because I didn't want to get married, I was just terrified. Announcing that you are getting married as a person who is gay is like a second coming out, so the fears are tangible. As much as I knew I had come a long way and had worked hard to move on from the messages I had told myself when I came out of the closet the first time, I was afraid that those messages (I am a failure; I am not good enough; I am not okay as I am; I am less than) would seep in again. Well, not so much seep in, but more so that I would let them in and believe them again. I was also worried about whether I could fully be myself on my wedding day even if there were a few people who couldn't completely support Clare and me. So I had been patient with myself, allowing myself enough space and time to be ready to get married. And then the day came. One morning, I woke up, I turned to Clare, and I said, "I'm ready." I knew I was strong enough and confident enough to embark on this journey with her.

I huffed and puffed over telling the first few family members, as I knew that would be the hardest — not because their reactions would be negative, but because I was overcoming something. Looking back, I feel like I was finding myself in a whole new way — marriage was something I wanted so deeply, but I had told myself I couldn't have it for so long that on some level I didn't think it could actually happen. As a result, its meaning had slipped from my fingertips as I longed to be the next straight couple who could jump through the ease of the traditional hoops laid before them — I didn't think I wanted to get married as a gay person, I told myself it wasn't important. But after telling my parents that we wanted to get married, I saw that the longing was still within me — and that all it needed was to be expressed. I could have it too! I was liberated. I was ecstatic! I was surprised at how elated I felt. My state of mind had shifted...about myself, about the world, about the way I thought magic occurred on this earth—that if you are patient, if you listen, if you follow your heart, eventually you will experience the joy that comes from suffering. And then I also saw that suffering would be no more—not in the way it had been.

By embracing myself and what I wanted, life had embraced me.

As we told more and more people about us getting married, their reactions went above and beyond, and any discomfort I had had with the idea settled with every new response. Yes, the idea of getting married to a woman is still an adjustment for me—years of cultural shaming play a part, I am sure. But it has seemed as though it has not been an adjustment for anyone else—just natural and genuine enthusiasm. Tears come to my eyes as I think about how grateful I am to those who have made this process special. They all confirmed what I had known deep down was possible —I had just never dared to dream I would actually see the day when I would feel such love in my heart coming in from the world outside of me—not because it hasn't tried to get in before but because I am letting it in now.

For the previous year during my meditation time, I would always find myself visualizing standing with Clare with all of our loved ones standing around us in a circle simply pouring their love and support into the moment. I can't say that I remember specific faces—it was more of a feeling that transcended what we typically experience on a daily basis. Its power was so overwhelming that when I would immerse myself in it I would become connected to the bigness of love and it was clear that I was a part of it—and every time I would be moved to tears because there was no better way to express that kind of adoration. Each time after meditating, I would think..."Maybe that is what I will get to experience when I die." But that time actually came on our wedding day.

I've never felt as free as I did on my wedding weekend. It was a surprise to me, as I had thought I would be more self-conscious. Well, I was self-conscious, but I was constantly pushing that part of me away. I was mostly nervous about kissing Clare in public, let alone in front of 50 other familiar faces. PDA has never been my thing. While I have been accepting of myself on one level, I have always felt challenged by displaying any sort of affection towards Clare in public. I am not talking about making out—but simple, loving gestures that imply we are a couple. If Clare and I are holding hands in our car in Mississippi and we stop next to another vehicle at a stop light that could *possibly* look in our window and see us holding hands—I let go. But something changed inside of me on my wedding weekend —I found myself reaching for Clare's hand in the crowds of Manhattan and putting my arm around her in front of my family and friends...a welcomed surprise.

I could feel the entire group of folks who made the trip to New York growing with me—stretching with me. In fact, the night before the wedding my cousin asked what we were going to be wearing for the ceremony. I answered, "White." I didn't want to give too much away. He then said, "Well, I've never done this before so I don't know what to expect." And I replied, "Me neither." There were no specific rules or traditions for us to follow going into it, so we made them up as we went along—and all somehow magically fell into place, as if it had already been written. A dream was unfolding that I didn't know I had dreamt.

After hanging out with family in the morning until lunchtime on our wedding day, we began to get ready for the ceremony. My mom said we held the record for brides getting ready—we were done in an hour's time. My mom did our make-up while we were listening to classical piano music —I needed the music to soothe the butterflies in my stomach. I felt like I was in the midst of finding a new part of myself through the process...consciously watching each minute, each moment float by while feeling both joy and anticipation. Appreciation and gratitude covered me with protection from any self-doubt. I was so deeply touched by those who had traveled to be with us and extremely overwhelmed with gratitude for those who had paved the way and made our marriage possible—I felt both infinitesimal and expansive at the same time.

Once we were ready, we caught a cab and picked up Clare's dad (a retired Episcopal bishop and our officiant) and his wife on our way to where we would be meeting everyone else for the ceremony—the Sixth Avenue entrance to Central Park. When we arrived, we were greeted by half our party, took pictures, signed our marriage license, and waited for the others to show. Once everyone showed up we were then going to walk into Central Park and find a spot to hold our ceremony.

As we waited, the clouds hovered above us—they had been threatening rain all day but had yet to follow through. However, the smell of rain was near, and not everyone had shown up to walk into the park with us. In the meantime, an old childhood friend took on the responsibility of finding us a spot in the park while we waited. She immediately happened upon one of the most popular wedding sights just 50 yards from where we were standing — and it was available. Another wedding was going to begin in 30 minutes, which was enough time for us to have our ceremony. Once everyone arrived, we made our way up a steep hill towards the beautiful gazebo covered with greenery. The steep hill instantly represented my own journey—climbing one step at a time away from fear and towards my own inner freedom. It was then we found ourselves surrounded in a circle by those we loved.

The ceremony was beautiful. During each pause I remember looking around at the eyes surrounding me, taking it in...letting it in. My eyes were filled with tears throughout the service—proof that love was overwhelming me. My dad read from 1st Corinthians, Clare's dad spoke on love and equality, we read our vows to one another and exchanged rings, and as Clare's dad was saying the final blessing and finals words, "What God has joined together let no man put asunder," it began to rain blessings upon our union. My mom stepped up behind me and sheltered Clare, me, and Clare's dad with her umbrella and put her arm around me as we all said the "Our Father" together, along with everyone else in attendance.

That prayer had never meant so much to me—not because of its words, but because of the unity it sparked. After the prayer, Clare's dad asked us to seal our commitment with a kiss. For once, I didn't pause to ponder the possible consequences of kissing a woman in public...I just acted as if my life had been waiting for me to choose a deeper truth over physicality. I chose truth without hesitation, and in that moment I was liberated from the shackles of my past. We went on to have a magnificent celebration that evening, full of toasts, laughter, dancing, and love. I'll never forget a moment of my wedding day.

Returning to Mississippi as a married woman has been a tougher transition than I had anticipated. Introducing Clare as my wife is a new challenge for me—another part of my healing that requires me to muster up courage each time, in order to let go of more fear and experience new levels of freedom. Yes, healing is a process, but that doesn't mean that moments of greatness won't appear along the way, and it certainly doesn't mean that a circle of love and support isn't always available—it is just quietly waiting for us to choose our truth so we can see it.

I know that you know what I know now. We all know. We are all capable of being both the person who is supportive and enthusiastic and the person who is willing to be poured into.

There is a deep part of me that knows what is true about life—that it is always faithful to the requests in our hearts, that grace is unpredictable in how it appears, that God is not out there somewhere—God is in here and everywhere—and that I am loved, and you are loved, so much.

Choose Courage

Creating Your
Heaven on Earth

by Meagan M. O'Nan

This uplifting book colorfully unveils such truths as the importance of love and accepting ourselves, the interconnectivity of us all, and how our thoughts and beliefs create our reality. Every one of us can create our heaven on earth.

"Creating Your Heaven on Earth is a comprehensive, easy-to-understand and life-changing book. This book helps us bring more love, trust, and joy into our lives. A must read." —Gary Quinn, author of Living in the Spiritual Zone

"This explorative book presents, captures and gives depth to the value and power the human spirit holds within us all. Creating Your Heaven on Earth will touch every soul it crosses." —Jamie Carey, U.S.A. Women's Basketball

"This is a book to read when you are in need of inspiration, feel downtrodden, fearful, doubt the truth of who you are or when you simply want to bask in the beauty of love. The saliency of choice shines through Meagan's words and point the way to truth." —Joan C. King, author of Cellular Wisdom series

CPSIA information can be obtained
at www.ICGtesting.com
Printed in the USA
BVHW041215241021
619364BV00009B/167